The Groom's Wedding Guidebook

Rayburn W. Ray & Rose Ann Ray

Revised Edition

©Copyright 1984, J M Publications, A Division of J M Productions, Incorporated. All rights reserved.

International copyright secured.

ISBN: 0-939298-22-8 (U.S.A.)

Printed in the United States of America

Third Printing

CONTENTS

Preface 1
1. Becoming Engaged 3
2. Planning With Your Fiancée 8
3. Planning With Your Family 13
4. Planning the Wedding Service 17
5. Obtaining Your License to Marry 21
6. Choosing Your Groomsmen 23
7. Compiling the Guest List 27
8. Assisting With Newspaper Announcements 31
9. Choosing Wedding Clothing 34
10. Entertaining and Being Entertained 37
11. Selecting Flowers 40
12. Giving and Receiving Gifts 42
13. Packing and Wardrobe Planning 45
14. Preserving the Memories 47
15. Planning the Rehearsal Dinner 51
16. Rehearsing Your Wedding 54
17. Enjoying the Wedding Day 56
18. Arranging a Memorable Honeymoon 61
19. Paying the Bills 66
20. Getting Settled 71
Timetable for the Groom 75

Dedicated to
Daniel and Mary Katharine
Who Planned Their Wedding Together

PREFACE
"Hey, I'm Getting Married Too"

Traditionally, about all that has been required of the bridegroom is to show up for the wedding. Such preoccupation with the bride led one neglected groom to utter in good-natured dismay, "Hey, I'm getting married too!" Indeed, each of the 2.4 million weddings performed last year in the United States required a willing groom as well as an ecstatic bride. Our own son and daughter were both recently married and, thus, became part of these statistics.

We have no desire to change the wedding day focus from the bride to the groom. However, we do feel that the disproportionate attention on the bride-to-be sometimes makes the prospective groom feel like a forgotten man. For example, when we shopped for an appropriate book for our son who had just become engaged, we couldn't find a single book addressed to the groom-to-be or his parents. Typically, one well-stocked bookstore had nothing for the groom, yet there were eight books for the bride or her parents, including our own recent book, *When Your Daughter Marries.*

A search of the Metropolitan Nashville Public Library failed to uncover a single volume in print specifically for the groom. This scarcity of wedding literature for the man is the principal reason for *The Groom's Wedding Guidebook.*

To the delight of their brides, both our son and future son-in-law chose to be very much involved in their wedding plans. We believe that most men getting married today, as perhaps never before, want to participate actively in their marriage plans—in spite of the conventional wisdom that the wedding day belongs to the bride. A traditionalist might counter that most wedding expenses are borne by the woman's family, thus entitling the bride to proceed with wedding preparations while the groom-to-be maintains a discreet silence. A little arithmetic will demolish this cost fantasy. While the groom and his family will not customarily pay as much for staging the wedding as the bride's family, the cost will likely equal out when the expense of a rehearsal dinner and a honeymoon is added. In fact, the cost of getting married will probably be greater for the man and his family when the cost of an engagement ring is included.

Whoever pays the bills, marriage at its best is a partnership—and that partnership might well begin with the engaged couple planning their wedding together. *The Groom's Wedding Guidebook* will assist you in planning with your fiancée and her parents as well as with your own parents. You'll also find help with the groom's primary concerns: planning the honeymoon, managing your money, and settling into your new home. Considerable attention is also given to how you can best comfort and support your bride as the wedding day draws near.

Congratulations as you approach the threshold of matrimony! Marriage is often berated, but this institution ordained of God remains far more fulfilling and enduring than any other human commitment. Our sincere hope is that *The Groom's Wedding Guidebook* will contribute to a happy, memorable occasion for you and your fiancée.

1
Becoming Engaged

Now that the woman of your dreams has said yes, you'll want to pause long enough to congratulate yourself! It's a tremendous compliment to a man when the woman he loves cares enough for him and trusts him enough to promise life-long devotion—as companion, lover, and partner.

If you're a man who likes a challenge, can you think of a greater one than becoming a husband who makes it easy for his wife to love, honor, and cherish him? Today's divorce statistics are a grim reminder that a blissful, enduring marriage can be achieved only by hard work and high commitment.

If your marriage is to be a genuine partnership, your active participation in the wedding plans and preparations will be an excellent beginning. Unfortunately, the groom-to-be is sometimes little more than a spectator at most of the pre-wedding activities. However, the wedding season will be far more meaningful and enjoyable if both you and your bride get caught up in the excitement and anticipation. And, why not? After all—you're getting married too! Along with the planning you'll do with your fiancée and your parents, there are several areas in which you'll need to take the initiative: buying an engagement ring, choosing your groomsmen, acquiring a marriage license, and arranging a honeymoon.

Telling Your Families

Your first business after her consent to marry you is to contact her parents. See them in person if at all possible. If they live a great distance away, you and your fiancée can telephone. If asking for her hand seems a trifle old-fashioned, permit her to break the news. You can then reassure her parents of your love for their daughter and your intention to take good care of her. You can then ask for their blessings on your marriage. Even if their approval is given reluctantly, you and your fiancée will be able to proceed with more confidence and calmness if this procedure is followed.

Chances are that you know how the news will be received. If you are expecting some problem, it might be better for your fiancée to tell her parents privately before you speak to them. You will then be better prepared to reassure them and to answer any questions they have about your ability to comfort and support their daughter. If you're a student or have just taken your first job, you'll do well to emphasize your career goals along with your present ability to support a wife.

Next, you'll need to tell your own parents. If your parents and your fiancée's parents do not know each other, your parents must take the initiative in arranging a meeting. If the two families are already acquainted, your parents should suggest a social occasion where the two families may plan informally for the big event. This get-together of parents may, of course, take place with or without you and your fiancée.

The announcement of the wedding should be made by the bride's parents three months before the wedding, if possible, but never less than six weeks before the date selected. The bride's family may wish to celebrate the official announcement with a party for the bride and you. If her family lives a great distance away, your parents may give the party. In any case, your parents will want to entertain their future daughter-in-law soon after they have learned of the engagement.

Your fiancée's family should send releases to newspapers in both communities if you do not live in the same city. You should telephone or write close friends and relatives if you want them to be aware of the wedding before they read about it in the newspaper.

Buying an Engagement Ring

The suitor who produces an engagement ring from his coat pocket the moment his sweetheart says "I will" hardly exists outside of the movies and story books. We do know of one resourceful young man who produced no less than three diamond rings with matching wedding bands when his girl agreed to marry him.

Yes, the diamonds were real—and no, the man was not a jewel thief! He was a college student who made a 700-mile journey to become engaged and he believed in being prepared. Fortunately, he had a cousin in the jewelry business who loaned him a selection of rings. Very romantic—but hardly your typical suitor.

These days, purchasing an engagement ring has become an event to be shared by both the man and the woman. You probably know already whether or not she wants a diamond. If you're not sure, it's not unromantic to ask her whether she prefers an expensive wedding band or a traditional engagement ring. Be honest with her if you don't have much money. In that case she might choose to wait for a diamond.

If you've decided to buy an engagement ring, set up an appointment with a jeweler you trust. Be sure to let him know beforehand what you can spend. That way, he'll be prepared to show your fiancée a good selection in your price range. Such a previous arrangement will avoid lots of "how much?—too much" conversation over the counter.

While you're in the jewelry store, you and your bride-to-be will want to examine wedding rings. Your fiancée will likely want to match her engagement ring, so it's a good idea to select them at the same time. You'll also want to arrange for engraving the wedding bands. Traditionally, wedding rings are engraved on the inside with the giver's initials first, then the receiver's initials and the date.

The jeweler can hold the wedding rings for later delivery, and will deliver the engagement ring to you so that you can put it on her finger in private at a suitable time. An appropriate time would be the day of the announcement party, if any, or the day your engagement becomes public information.

There is, of course, no substitute for a jeweler you trust, but the selection of the rings will go more smoothly if you know a few basics about diamonds. The value of a diamond is not determined by size alone, but by four distinct characteristics known in the trade as the "four C's"—color, cut, clarity and carat.

Color—Pure white and blue-white diamonds are very rare and expensive. Other usable shades are yellow, coffee brown, pink, red, black, and green. Tinges of yellow, brown or black will reduce a stone's value.

Cut—Most diamonds are cut to have fifty-eight facets, transforming them into a prism that breaks up light into all colors of the spectrum. A perfectly cut diamond will reflect all the light upwards for maximum brilliance. Cut also refers to shape and is a matter of personal preference. The five shapes are round or brilliant, oval, pear, marquise, and emerald.

Clarity—Since a flawless diamond is extremely rare, the important question is whether an imperfection or inclusion affects stability, clarity or brilliance. To prove the clarity of a diamond, it should be examined under a jeweler's glass powerful enough to magnify it ten times. Any impurity that can't be seen at that magnification will not detract from its value or durability.

Carat—This is the unit of weight used for diamonds. One carat equals one-fifth of a gram. A diamond is usually priced according to its size as well as the number, kind, and location of its inclusions.

While the diamond is the traditional engagement ring, other precious stones such as emeralds, rubies, or sapphires may be used. Your bride-to-be may actually prefer a jewelled necklace or bracelet to a ring.

How much should you expect to pay for an engagement ring? According to the National Bridal Service, 87 percent of the brides in America receive an engagement ring with an average cost of over $500. Many bridal consultants suggest an amount be spent equal to six weeks to two months pay. This amount will likely be greater than many young grooms can afford.

In this situation, you can expect your girl to be more sentimental than mercenary. She may be delighted with your grandmother's opal or another family heirloom. As one father told his son, "If she wants to marry you, she should be just as happy with a ring from a bubble gum machine as a ring from the Tiffany collection." While this father had a valid point, you'll probably want to buy her the best ring you can afford.

A Ring for You

You can select a wedding band for yourself to match hers, or you may choose a different type entirely. Some men are now receiving engagement rings from their fiancées which may be worn on a finger other than the traditional ring finger. Colored stones, such as birthstones, are a popular choice. If you would like to have an engagement ring, let your jeweler know—and drop a hint to your bride-to-be.

Charting Life for Two

Along with immediate planning for the wedding with your fiancée and your parents (to be discussed in the next two chapters), you must tackle such practical concerns as where you'll live and how your lives and possessions can be merged in the most satisfying fashion. While some decisions can be deferred until after the honeymoon, you'll feel better if you can tie down as many as possible *before* the wedding.

In charting life for two, the two most pressing questions are where you will live and how you will be able to live on your resources. If either of you is still in school, you'll likely be on a tight budget. However small or large your resources, you and your bride will need to work out a realistic household budget.

If you're moving into a new house or apartment, you'll probably need to arrange for utilities. You'll want to examine your insurance needs with a reliable agent. Homeowner's insurance will be needed if you're fortunate enough to own a house or condominium. Otherwise, you'll want a renter's policy on your possessions. If you or your fiancée is presently listed as a dependent on a family health policy, coverage will likely cease thirty days after your marriage.

You may also need trip insurance for your honeymoon, and if both of you will be driving the same automobile both must be listed on the policy. You should also be thinking about your life insurance needs. You may require additional coverage as well as changing the beneficiary of existing policies.

Along with your household budget, your financial planning should include one or more checking accounts and a savings program. These and other business matters will be dealt with in Chapter 20, "Getting Settled."

2
Planning With Your Fiancée

Planning the wedding with your fiancée can be fun and can actually draw you closer together. However, if you assume that planning the wedding is the business of the bride and her parents, the festivities may end up disappointing you. Don't pass up the opportunity to involve yourself in the wedding decisions and arrangements. Remember, you are the co-star of this unfolding marital drama.

Choosing the Kind of Wedding

First, decide the size and type of wedding the two of you want. Should it be a very formal evening ceremony with several attendants and a large guest list? A somewhat formal afternoon wedding? Perhaps you would prefer a more informal ceremony attended mainly by your families and close friends. Chances are that you have already discussed this.

The main consideration is to be completely honest with each other. If you don't want a big wedding, now is the time to express yourself. If you feel that a relatively expensive formal wedding is inconsistent with your means or lifestyle, let this be known. Don't vacillate about whatever you agree to, however. Keep in mind that the bride's family is the traditional wedding host and, ideally, the wishes of the bride and her parents should be carried out. As sponsors of the wedding, they will probably be paying most of the bills.

The formality of your wedding is determined by time of day, wedding attire, number of attendants, size of guest list, and the general ambience of the wedding site. Weddings after six P.M. tend to be more formal than daytime ceremonies.

At a very formal evening wedding, the bride wears an elaborate full-length gown with long train and veil. The groom and his men wear "white tie and tails" or other suitable formal wear. At an ultra-formal wedding, guests may be asked to wear "black tie." Such a wedding would likely have 150 or more guests, six or more attendants each for the bride and groom, and an elaborate reception.

For the very formal daytime wedding, the bridal gown may be somewhat less elaborate. The groom would likely wear a black or a grey cutaway with striped trousers. Again, there may be six or more attendants and a sizable guest list.

At the less formal night wedding, the bride's ensemble is less extravagant than at the very formal evening ceremony. The groom may wear the tuxedo of his choice in black, grey, brown, or more contemporary colors. An alternative would be a formal dinner jacket with matching or coordinated trousers and vest. This type of ceremony would probably have three to six attendants and more than one hundred guests.

For the less formal daytime wedding, the bride may wear a more simple gown, floor length or with a short or chapel train. The groom may wear a tuxedo, stroller or an appropriate business suit. Again there would be three to six attendants and one hundred or more guests.

At the informal wedding, the bride may choose a suit or street-length dress, and the groom would wear a business suit. The bride and groom would have one or two attendants each, and the wedding might be attended only by the two families and a few close friends.

Selecting the Date

After choosing the size and type of wedding, you and your fiancée should decide on the month or season for the big event. You will probably need to do some checking before setting the exact date and hour for the ceremony. Your own preferences and the convenience of the guests should be the main considerations in setting the time and place of the wedding. While it is not possible to please everyone, try to avoid obvious conflicts.

Deciding on the Place

Where will you have the wedding? The size of the event and the atmosphere the two of you want should be primary considerations. According to the National Bridal Service, eighty-eight percent of the weddings in America are held at a church or synagogue. Possibilities usually include the church sanctuary, a smaller chapel, and the minister's study.

Other wedding sites are a hotel or hall, a club, or a home. Home and club weddings are often held in a garden setting, particularly in the summer.

As soon as a tentative date and a desired location are chosen, the bride or her mother should contact the church or hall representative to reserve the site. The reservation will have to be tentative until they learn if the minister or other officiant is available.

Choosing the Officiant

Choice of the officiant is the prerogative of the bride, but she will want to be sure you are happy with her selection. The person chosen should be contacted as soon as possible to confirm his availability at the time and place desired. It is a good idea to have one or two alternate dates in mind in case the minister is not available at the preferred time.

If the wedding is to be held at the bride's church, the minister is customarily called on for assistance. He will be familiar with local customs and any requirements or restrictions imposed by the church. The bride's pastor is the logical choice as main officiant unless there is good reason to depart from this practice. The groom's pastor often takes part in the service also.

The pastor will honor the bride's wishes if she has chosen another minister to officiate or assist him with the service. Don't hesitate to suggest that your minister be asked to assist with the ceremony if this is your desire. The main officiant will suggest ways in which the service can be shared satisfactorily.

You and the bride will want to discuss your attendants. Ideally, each of you should have the same number of attendants, but this is not absolutely essential. In addition to your best man, you will need an usher for every forty or fifty guests.

This is also the time to talk about the role of family members in the wedding party. Along with the participation of your own family members, you may want to use the bride's brother as an usher, and the bride may choose your sister as a bridesmaid.

Conferring with the Minister

The two of you will likely discuss general plans for the ceremony at the first conference with the minister or other officiant. He will need to know whether a single or double ring ceremony will be needed. If another minister is to assist in the service, plans must be made for his participation.

You and the bride must decide if you want a traditional ceremony with a few personal touches or if you desire a more contemporary service. You may want to memorize your vows or even compose your own. This kind of participation can be impressive if done well. You'll also need to discuss the music to be used at the ceremony. (See Chapter 4 "Planning the Wedding Service.")

The minister will probably want to go ahead and schedule a rehearsal for the wedding. He'll likely ask for one or more conferences to complete plans for the ceremony and to discuss the spiritual significance of your marriage.

Financing the Wedding

It is most important that you and your fiancée and each of your parents understand clearly how the wedding will be financed. While there is a traditional consensus on who pays for what, there are few binding rules. The main consideration is that no one goes broke paying for the wedding. If either you or the bride is well-established financially, one of you may be in a better position than your parents to pay for certain items. Any arrangement is appropriate that is mutually satisfactory to all parties. Some families even decide to divide all expenses equally.

Generally, the bride's family assumes responsibility for virtually everything related to the ceremony itself except the minister's fee and certain floral bouquets and boutonnieres that are paid for by the groom. The bride's family should host the reception if at all possible, but the rehearsal dinner is often given by the groom's family. The honeymoon is the responsibility of the groom, but he may accept the wedding trip as a gift from either side of the family.

Every member of the wedding party is responsible for his or her own wedding clothing. You and the bride should each provide lodging for your out-of-town attendants. Attendants pay for their transportation to the wedding site, but you and your fiancée furnish transportation to wedding activities as needed.

Staying in Touch

You will want to stay in close touch with your bride-to-be throughout the wedding season and do your part to keep her happy and composed. Getting ready for a wedding can be fun for a bride, but may grow hectic at times, particularly if she must work or attend classes until shortly before the event. It's not unusual for either of you to develop doubts as the wedding day approaches. Your support and understanding at this time will strengthen your relationship and help build a solid foundation for your marriage.

You'll be wise to arrange for vacation time from work for a few days *before* the wedding, particularly if you're not located where you're getting married. You can leisurely organize things and enjoy spending time with your family and friends. Being on hand will also please your fiancée. As one recent bride put it, "It saves the bride from "too-much-to-do" panic if the groom is available."

3
Planning With Your Family

Your wedding is a most important occasion in the life of your parents. They have nurtured you through the years and have deep feelings about this exciting venture. They look forward with joy and some trepidation to the time of the wedding, wondering what the role of the groom's parents may be and what they can do to help you. Also they look back on the years of family togetherness and consider changes that will be taking place in their relationship with you.

After you and your fiancée have agreed on the wedding plans, both sets of parents will be informed of the joyous occasion. If you live in the same town as your parents, you and your fiancée might drop by to give the good news. If you believe your announcement will come as something of a surprise to your parents, you could go by alone to tell them of your plans and then have the bride and your parents get together for supper or a visit.

If you live out of town, you can telephone with the news and explain all the details of when and where. The call might be followed up with a letter, telling again of your plans, the important dates, and especially how important your parents' support will be to you in the months to come.

If the two families live in the same city, your parents will want to invite the bride's parents over for dinner or for coffee and dessert. At this occasion, your mother may want to give your fiancée an engagement gift such as a piece of jewelry or a family heirloom. If the bride's family lives too far away for your family to entertain them, your mother should write a warm and friendly note.

Discussing Finances

If you are established in a job, your parents will probably contribute less financially to the expenses of the wedding than if you are a student or a new graduate. You will still want to discuss with your parents the costs of the wedding and what share they wish to assume. The rehearsal dinner is the largest single expense usually assumed by the groom's parents.

If your family is much better off financially than the bride's family, you or your parents might tactfully offer to assume some expenses that would normally be paid by the bride's family. For instance, your family might offer to pay for one-half of the total flower bill or pay the postage for the invitations.

Involving Your Family

Your family may feel that most of the excitement and decisions revolve around the bride and her family—and that is quite true. Your folks will feel more a part of the action, however, if some general wedding plans are discussed with them and their opinions are asked. You and your fiancée could get feedback from them on clothing for the groomsmen, music, flowers, and general wedding plans.

Your father may not express the same keen level of interest as your mother in all aspects of the wedding, but he will appreciate being asked his ideas on photography, taping the wedding, and even the music.

Often a father or brother is asked to be best man. One groom who chose his father as best man wrote from his college campus to his parents, "Dad, thanks for agreeing to be my best man. I can't think of anyone who's had a greater influence on me or been closer. It's too bad I can't have a best lady too, huh, Mom!"

Your mother will not be an official member of the wedding party, but she will find much to do supporting your plans. She will appreciate seeing swatches of material for the bridesmaids' dresses or giving some suggestions on songs for the ceremony. Consult with the bride so you can let your mother know which of the family's friends have accepted or had to decline the wedding invitation.

Your fiancée may ask your sister to be one of her bridesmaids. Your brother may serve as a groomsman. At dinner or parties, your family will propose toasts, circulate among the guests, and support all activities by their presence if at all possible.

If you have brothers or sisters living at home, most likely they will be eager to give a hand with the wedding plans. They can help spruce up the house with a coat of paint, plant a flower bed or wax the family car.

Your mother, after checking with your fiancée's mother, will choose her gown for the wedding. She will follow the lead of the bride's mother in length, degree of formality, and appropriate color. Your father, if not in the wedding party, may choose to wear a dark business suit. However, he may prefer to dress the same as other men in the party since he will be in the receiving line.

Your mother and sisters may wish to give a luncheon or tea honoring the bride and introducing her to their friends. This could be at a local hotel, or in the home, perhaps as a patio party or barbecue.

Include your grandparents in your plans. They will also be invited to parties and festivities. Maybe they would like to entertain for you—such as having the groomsmen over for a country breakfast.

As your groomsmen and friends arrive from out of town, your parents could arrange a supper at a restaurant or perhaps a simple but hearty meal at home. Your groomsmen may be able to stay in the homes of family friends since it is your responsibility to provide lodging for members of your wedding party. Your friends would be happy to know there are always fixings for sandwiches or a quick snack at your parents' home.

Attending Bridal Functions

Your parents will probably receive invitations throughout the wedding season for parties in honor of the bridal couple. Let them know that you appreciate their making the effort to attend every one they possibly can.

Your parents, sisters, and brothers can help you compile the invitation list that you will give to the bride and her parents. They will have names and addresses of family, church, neighborhood, and business friends. Perhaps your brothers and sisters can help you locate contemporaries through school yearbooks, office directories, alumni journals, etc.

If you are living at home or college or even if you have an apartment, you probably have some clothes and boxes of mementos, class notes, and other papers at your parents' home. An afternoon spent going through these things, throwing away and consolidating what you wish to keep would be appreciated by your parents as well as being helpful to you.

After the ceremony, it would be a nice gesture for your mother to write to the mother of the bride expressing delight and appreciation for the lovely wedding.

4
Planning the Wedding Service

You and your fiancée will want to make your wedding service as meaningful and memorable as possible. This will likely mean a blending of traditions—old and new—with unique personal touches.

Selecting the Ceremony

You and the bride-to-be will likely select the type of wedding ceremony you want at the first conference with the minister or other officiant. Whatever form of ceremony is chosen, the wedding service should be viewed as a whole—words, music, flowers and symbolism blending into a happy, meaningful union of your lives.

Civil ceremonies are usually extremely short with emphasis on the legal and social aspects of the marriage. The content of the ceremony may include little more than the couple's response to questions about the seriousness of their intentions, the exchanging of vows and rings, and the pronouncement by the official.

Weddings performed by a minister usually include an opening statement on the sanctity of marriage, appropriate instrumental music, relevant Bible passages and prayers, the giving or presenting of the bride, the exchanging of vows, the giving and receiving of rings, and a final pronouncement that the couple are "husband and wife."

A unity candle is now being used in some services to represent the union of the couple's lives in marriage. With small lighted candles, the bride and groom simultaneously light the large unity candle. A variation calls for the parents of the bride and groom to participate in the lighting, thus symbolizing the joining of the two families as well as the couple.

Most traditional weddings in Protestant churches use a ceremony that is a variation of the Episcopal wedding service that begins, "Dearly beloved, we are gathered here in the sight of God and this company to join together this man and this woman in holy matrimony."

If you and the bride agree on this type of service, the two of you will be relieved of worry about the mechanics of the ceremony until the rehearsal. The minister will direct the questions and lead in the responses at the appropriate time. This arrangement is the simplest because it places no responsibility on the bride and groom to remember cues or memorize vows. This procedure is recommended if either of you expects to be nervous about the ceremony. Little can go wrong with an experienced minister directing the ceremony.

If you prefer to memorize your vows or compose your own, be sure such an arrangement is agreeable with the minister. He will likely have helpful suggestions for personalizing your wedding. A good sound system will be needed for the vows to be properly heard and appreciated in a large auditorium.

Couples interested in composing their vows will find the *Wedding Ceremony Idea Book* by George W. Knight extremely helpful. If not available in your Christian bookstore, the book can be ordered from J M Productions, P. O. Box 837, Brentwood, Tennessee 37027.

In formulating the service, Knight advises to remember the principle of balance. "Try to balance every new and innovative feature with some traditional element that will be instantly recognized by your wedding guests. Otherwise you might end up with a ceremony so modern and radical that it comes across as cold and unfeeling. Remember that human beings find security in the familiar. Your object should be to strike a happy balance between the old and the new as you plan the service."

Choosing Music and Musicians

The selection of music and musicians is vital to creating the right atmosphere for the wedding. Appropriate music, beautifully performed, helps to establish a mood of both solemnity and joy for the marriage ceremony.

You and the bride will first need to determine whether you favor classical wedding music, hymns and church anthems, or contemporary songs. Perhaps a combination of religious and popular music will be most satisfactory. Do you prefer all instrumental music or vocal selections by a soloist or a vocal group? How will the music be integrated in the ceremony?

If help is needed in choosing suitable music, ask your bride's church organist, choir director or a musician friend to suggest some possibilities. Most Protestant churches will permit both religious and popular music, but check with the minister to be sure your choice is appropriate for the service, particularly if secular music is favored.

Many brides and grooms like a selection of both popular and church music for their wedding. It is usually better to use the contemporary songs either before the ceremony starts or early in the wedding, reserving the more solemn or inspirational music for the climax of the service. We attended an impressive wedding in which the couple had chosen several popular love songs to be played before the mothers were seated. The music used during the ceremony itself was more traditional in nature.

You and the bride will almost certainly want an organist even if no other musicians are used. Most traditional ceremonies at a church or chapel begin with a soft prelude lasting about a half hour while guests are seated. Aside from the prelude and accompanying the vocalists, the organist will provide the processional as the wedding party enters the church, a recessional as they leave the altar, and a lively postlude as guests file out.

The most logical choice for the wedding musician is the church's organist. He or she will be familiar with the instrument and will likely be an experienced wedding musician. A pianist may be used instead of or in addition to the organist. If you or the bride have a relative or friend who is an accomplished musician, you may want to use that person. If you have difficulty finding a musician, ask for suggestions from churches or local high schools and colleges.

Popular processional choices are the "Bridal Chorus" from

Lohengrin by Wagner and "Trumpet Voluntary" by Clark.

Music can be used very creatively in an otherwise traditional ceremony. At a wedding in a college chapel, a violinist performed from a balcony as the wedding party proceeded to the altar. In a church ceremony, the service was climaxed by selections from an unseen choral group in the balcony.

A groom who was a talented soloist sang to his bride at an appropriate place in the ceremony. Another groom, who taught music at a nearby college, composed a song in honor of his bride, and the organist performed the selection for the first time at the wedding. Congregational singing is being increasingly used as a means of including guests in the wedding celebration.

Since the wedding ceremony is normally quite short, we suggest using a talented soloist, choral group, or string quartet in addition to the organist or pianist. They will bring added pleasure to the guests and give special meaning to the ceremony. These musicians, whether professionals or close friends, should be able to perform in a near-professional manner. Church and school musicians are not likely to be as costly as other professional musicians. In fact, some church choral groups may be willing to perform without pay.

Just after the bride's mother has been seated is an appropriate time for a soloist or choir to sing, or for a small ensemble to perform. Traditional favorites that might be used here include, "O Promise Me," "Because," "I Love You Truly," "The Wedding Song," and "Till the End of Time."

The time between the giving of the bride and the exchanging of vows is also suitable for a solo or other musical selection. Any music at this stage of the wedding should complement the ceremony as much as possible. For example, a soloist sang "How Do I Love Thee?" after a minister had commented on the popular love passage from 1 Corinthians 13:4–8.

Many couples choose a solo or choral benediction as they kneel at the altar just prior to the pronouncement. A long-time favorite is Malotte's "The Lord's Prayer." "The Wedding March" by Mendelssohn is a popular choice for the recessional.

5
Obtaining Your License to Marry

Every state requires a marriage license, which is usually purchased at your local county clerk's office. Most of these offices are closed on weekends and holidays.

If you're in a hurry to tie the knot, no other state offers the convenience of Nevada. There is no blood test and no waiting period — and you can buy a marriage license until midnight during the week and around the clock on weekends.

In Las Vegas the wedding may be performed at any hour by a wedding commissioner in a small office or by a minister-on-call at a wedding chapel. A short civil ceremony in this desert oasis may cost as little as $50 and take about ten minutes.

Readers of this guidebook will doubtless be interested in a wedding that is more deliberate and ceremonial.

Most states require proof that you and your fiancée are of age or have parental consent to marry. You will need evidence of citizenship if either of you were born outside the United States. You will almost certainly need doctor's certificates verifying the results of any necessary blood tests or physical examinations. Incidentally, this is a good time to get a complete physical and dental examination.

There is often a waiting period of two or three days before the license is valid, and the license is good for a maximum period of usually fifteen to thirty days.

You'll want to check on the requirements for a license and the hours when it may be purchased. Keep any waiting periods in mind when you make a date to get the license. If you and your bride-to-be are a working couple, why not take a half-day off, and afterward, celebrate with a long lunch at a favorite restaurant.

If your wedding trip will take you out of the country, you'll need to check on passports, visas, and inoculations.

6
Choosing Your Groomsmen

In less civilized times, the groom and his men swept down upon the residents of a rival village and carried off the fairest maiden. The groom's men fought off the aroused villagers. The role of groomsmen is less arduous today, but they are still central figures in your wedding drama.

The bride will choose a maid or matron of honor and bridesmaids. You are responsible for selecting approximately the same number of groomsmen along with your best man.

The term "groomsmen" is sometimes used to describe all the men in the wedding party except the groom. Strictly speaking, however, your groomsmen are those who "stand up" with you at the altar.

At most weddings, the groomsmen consist of the best man and ushers who take their place at the altar. At an exceptionally large wedding, two to four additional men may be selected to serve only as ushers.

Selecting the Best Man and Ushers

If you've not chosen your best man already, he should be the friend or family member you'll be most comfortable with at the altar. He should also be available and willing to be your confidant and chief assistant throughout the wedding festivities. Logical choices are your best friend, your brother, or perhaps your father.

If you have two people you want to honor as "best men," it is perfectly proper for you to have two attendants in the same fashion as the bride who has two honor attendants. We attended a large formal wedding in which both the bride and the groom had two honor attendants. The bride used her two sisters as maid and matron of honor while the groom was attended by his father and his brother.

For most weddings you'll need one usher for every forty or fifty guests. You'll want to choose your groomsmen from close friends and relatives. It's also a nice gesture to use the bride's brother. While it is ideal to have the same number of ushers as bridesmaids, this arrangement may not be practical. It is perfectly permissible for two men or two women to walk together in the recessional.

You should contact the men chosen to serve in your wedding as soon as possible after the date is set. They will need to know about dress requirements and about related wedding activities they'll be expected to attend.

Your friends may need time to check their calendars to make certain there is no unavoidable conflict. It is sometimes necessary for a close friend to decline the honor though he would very much like to be in your wedding.

Defining Duties of the Best Man

As the name implies, the groom's *best* man should combine the qualities of a trusted companion, nurse, and valet. It's the best man's duty to keep the groom calm and on schedule. He is virtually the chief of staff at the wedding, toastmaster at the reception, and personal aide to the groom.

He bears responsibility for the groom being properly dressed and on time for the ceremony and other wedding functions. He sees that the ceremony officiant is paid and takes charge of the marriage license and the bride's wedding ring. He may also supervise the ushers, making sure that they are properly dressed, thoroughly briefed, and at the wedding site on time.

The best man coordinates plans for the bachelor dinner and usually serves as emcee at the rehearsal dinner. He sits to the right of the bride at the reception and proposes the first toast to the new couple. He sees that all goes well at the reception and that no harmful jokes are played on the couple. For example, he'll intervene if pranksters try to disable the newlyweds' car or obstruct its windshield.

This key member of the wedding party helps the newlyweds embark on their honeymoon. He assists the groom with last minute packing and takes care of the luggage. He accompanies the couple as they leave the reception or drives them off, delivering keys, reservations, etc. given him for safekeeping. He is often designated to see that all rental clothing is returned promptly to the store. He may even be asked to send a telegram in the groom's name to his new in-laws expressing appreciation for the wedding.

Identifying Duties of the Ushers

Ushers should arrive at the wedding site an hour before the ceremony, properly dressed, and with boutonnieres in place. They usually take their place as groomsmen at the altar and serve as escorts for the bridesmaids during the recessional. They should also give whatever assistance is requested by the groom or the best man.

As the guests arrive, an usher steps forward and offers his arm to each woman. If he does not know her and she does not present a pew card, he asks her if she is a friend of the bride or the groom and seats her accordingly. The bride's guests are usually seated on the left and the groom's on the right. (Guests may be seated on either side if one side is expected to have considerably more guests than the other). When a man and a woman arrive together, the woman takes the usher's arm and the man follows them down the aisle.

If several women appear together, the eldest is seated first. A man alone, unless he is elderly and in need of assistance, may simply be accompanied to his seat by an usher. Ushers should make polite conversation with guests as they walk down the aisle.

The groom should designate a head usher to supervise the seating of guests. Seating will proceed more smoothly if ushers will make notes at the rehearsal of special seating arrangements. If one of the ushers is the brother of the bride or groom, he will probably escort his own mother to her seat. Otherwise the head usher will assume responsibility for the mothers. If an aisle carpet is used, the groom appoints two ushers to unroll it. Ushers are normally designated to light and extinguish candles at the appointed time.

It's a gracious gesture to have an usher stand just outside the door of each entrance to the church to greet and open the door for guests as they arrive. It's also a good idea to assign one or two ushers to the entrance of the reception area to greet and instruct guests as they arrive.

During the reception, ushers sit at the bridal table and often propose toasts to the bride and groom. They do not stand in the receiving line but circulate among guests during much of the reception. Ushers should make a special effort to see that everyone, including the bridesmaids, has a good time at the reception.

7
Compiling the Guest List

The bride and her family are responsible for coordinating the guest list and issuing the wedding invitations. First of all, they must decide how many guests can be accommodated comfortably.

Traditionally, the guest list is divided equally between the bride's family and the groom's. However, if the groom's family is from out of town, his family would require fewer invitations. Another plan is to divide the invitations by thirds among the two families and the couple themselves.

Contributing to the Guest List

Whichever plan is used, you and your parents will have the opportunity to help compile the guest list. While addresses may not be necessary at the outset, it will be very helpful to have a list of names to determine the number of invitations needed and the size reception hall required.

Who should be included on the groom's invitation list? First, consider who *must* be invited. Begin by listing your attendants and their spouses or fiancées. Parents of the attendants should be invited. If your minister is taking part in the ceremony, be sure to include him and his wife.

Next, list family members and other relatives (by households) who are not in the wedding party. Names of children under eighteen who are to be invited should be listed under the parents' names. If a friend or fiancée of an unmarried guest is to be invited, the person should receive a separate invitation rather than being addressed as "and escort." Young people eighteen or older receive their own invitations, even if they are living in the parents' home.

Others who may be invited are church and school friends, distant relatives, neighbors, business associates, fellow club members, and children of close friends and relatives. If you must reduce your guest list, it is best to decrease it by categories.

For example, you might want to exclude all casual business acquaintances unless you're planning to invite everyone in town. It's better to leave out an entire group such as all small children, distant cousins, or neighbors of your parents than to slight some members of each group.

Where can you find addresses for the guest list? Try telephone directories, employee rosters, alumni publications, church directories, club yearbooks, and Christmas card lists. Perhaps a friend who has recently married can supply you with addresses of hard-to-locate friends.

In compiling your final guest list, you can expedite everything by alphabetizing the names and typing names and addresses exactly as the envelopes should be prepared. Be sure to write out all titles except Mr., Mrs., Ms., Jr., and Dr. It is best not to use initials or nicknames. Streets and cities are written in full with no abbreviations. Don't forget the zip code.

The more complete your list, the less likelihood of an error when your list is consolidated with that of the bride's family. Prepare your list as early as possible so that invitations may be delivered from the printer in time to send out four to six weeks before the ceremony.

Helping Select an Invitation

The bride will likely want your help in selecting the style and wording of the wedding invitation. There are, of course, many styles of both traditional and contemporary invitations. The conventional invitation may be worded as follows:

> Mr. and Mrs. Winston Allen Johnson
> request the honour of your presence
> at the marriage of their daughter
> Melanie Ann

to
Mr. David William Reynolds
on Saturday, the tenth of September
nineteen hundred and eighty-three
at five o'clock
First Methodist Church
Greenville, South Carolina

Your fiancée may suggest that your parents' names be included on the invitation. There are basically two ways in which your parents may be listed on the invitation along with the bride's parents.

One possibility is to have the invitation issued jointly by the parents of the bride and the parents of the groom. Incidentally, the names appearing at the top of the invitation refer to who is sponsoring the wedding, not necessarily to who is paying for it. An invitation signifying joint sponsorship might look like this:

Mr. and Mrs. Walter Frank Campbell
and
Mr. and Mrs. George Evans Appleton
request the honour of your presence
at the marriage uniting their children
Deborah Jane
and
John Mark
on Friday, the eighth of July
nineteen hundred and eighty-three
at seven o'clock in the evening
Calvary Baptist Church
Baton Rouge, Louisiana

The names of your parents may also appear on the invitation as an honor whether they are co-sponsoring the wedding or not. The traditional invitation would then be worded:

Mr. and Mrs. Walter Frank Campbell
request the honour of your presence
at the marriage of their daughter
Deborah Jane
to

Mr. John Mark Appleton
son of
Mr. and Mrs. George Evans Appleton
on Friday, the eighth of July
nineteen hundred and eighty-three
at seven o'clock in the evening
Calvary Baptist Church
Baton Rouge, Louisiana

The bride may want a picture of the two of you on the front of the invitation. Such a picture may be in color or in black and white and may be used along with traditional or contemporary wording. The photographs are frequently oval in shape. This type of invitation may serve to introduce the bride or groom in instances where either is not known to some of the guests. The picture invitation may also become a valued keepsake.

8
Assisting With Newspaper Announcements

The bride or her mother may need your assistance in preparing appropriate information for newspaper announcements of your engagement and the wedding. If you and your fiancée live in different cities, it may be more convenient for you or your parents to handle the announcement in your local newspaper.

Announcing the Engagement

Announcements of the engagement in newspapers and other publications serve to publicize the upcoming wedding and to remind invited guests of the big event. Clippings also provide excellent souvenirs for scrapbooks and the bride's memory box.

The newspaper's society editor should be contacted about any special requirements for the announcement and the bridal picture. Larger newspapers often provide a form requesting information needed for the write-up. A black and white glossy photograph at least 5 x 7 in size is preferred by most publications.

Newspapers in cities with more than one daily paper may require that the engagement announcement appear exclusively in their publication. Some newspapers will use only one picture of the bride during the wedding season, so a choice must be made between an engagement picture and a picture accompanying the wedding announcement. Some newspapers will accept a picture of the couple with the engagement announcement while others will use only photographs of the bride.

Since the large newspaper will likely have a backlog of announcements during the peak wedding months, it is a good idea to provide the information and the picture as much as two months before the ceremony. The bride can arrange with the wedding photographer to take an advance picture in her wedding gown, or another picture may be used.

The smaller newspaper will welcome a prepared announcement that requires a minimum of editing. They will also be pleased to have a bridal picture. The announcement should be typed and double-spaced and include a name and phone number in case the newspaper wants more information.

The following is a typical announcement which can be adapted for most publications:

Glasscock-Ray

The engagement of Miss Mary Katharine Glasscock to Daniel George Ray is announced by her parents, Mr. and Mrs. Burnard Glasscock of Shelbyville, Tennessee. He is the son of Mr. and Mrs. Rayburn W. Ray of Nashville.

Granddaughter of Mr. and Mrs. A. M. Deering and of the late Mr. and Mrs. E. L. Glasscock, the future bride is a graduate of Central High School in Shelbyville. She received a bachelor of science degree from Tennessee Technological University where she served as vice-president of Kappa Delta sorority and held membership in Sigma Tau Delta.

The bridegroom is the grandson of Mrs. Rose T. Collier and of the late Mr. and Mrs. Morgan Wood Ray. A graduate of McGavock High School in Nashville, he attended The University of the South. He is a graduate of Tennessee Tech, where he served as president of Phi Gamma Delta. He will begin a master of business administration program in the fall at Tech.

The wedding will take place on September 12 at St. William's Catholic Church in Shelbyville.

Announcing the Wedding

Most newspapers will carry an announcement of the wedding along with a picture of the bride and groom if supplied to the publication within two weeks of the wedding. Check with the newspaper before the ceremony about their requirements.

Ray-Klein Are Wed

Jennifer Ann Ray and Mark Stefan Klein were married on Saturday, September 12, at First Baptist Church in Nashville.

She is the daughter of Mr. and Mrs. Rayburn W. Ray of Nashville, and he is the son of Mr. and Mrs. Dick O. Klein of Northfield, Illinois.

Dr. Franklin Paschall officiated at the 2 p. m. ceremony, assisted by Mr. Ray. Nuptial music was presented by Richard Brown, organist, and David Ford, soloist.

Mr. Ray gave his daughter in marriage. She wore a candlelight chiffon bridal gown made in the empire style with petal sleeves and a bodice trimmed with alencon lace. The mantilla shoulder-length veil of chiffon was edged with alencon lace. She carried a bouquet of sonia roses, white carnations, baby's breath, and fujii pompons.

Serving as matron of honor was Mrs. Robert S. DuFresne, Jr. of Chicago. The maid of honor was Miss Nora Frances Stone of Columbus, Mississippi. Bridesmaids were Miss Laura Barker of Birmingham, Miss Cindy Boatwright of New York, Mrs. Debbie Mader of Birmingham, and Miss Sallie Roper of Durham, North Carolina.

The attendants wore A-line gowns of peach blossom chiffon and carried nosegays of sonia roses, peach carnations, daisies, and baby's breath.

Rock Klein of Washington, D. C., the groom's brother, served as best man. Other groomsmen were: Lauren Harsted of Phoenix; Dan Kendree of Phoenix; Greg Klein, the groom's brother, from Chicago; David Luhr of Los Angeles; and Daniel Ray, the bride's brother, from Nashville.

A reception was given in the church parlor following the ceremony.

The bridal couple took a wedding trip to Isle of Palms and Charleston, South Carolina. They will live in Chicago, where the bride is feature editor of *Modern Salon* magazine and the groom is an account executive with the Leo Burnett advertising agency.

9
Choosing Wedding Clothing

The type of wedding you and your fiancée have agreed on will largely dictate what you and your groomsmen will wear. Considerations bearing on your choice of wedding attire will be: (1) the degree of formality desired; (2) the setting of the ceremony; (3) the time of day; (4) the season of the year; and, (5) local custom.

All men in the wedding party, including the bride's father, should dress essentially the same. The neckwear and boutonnieres of the groom and best man may be different to distinguish them from the other men.

In most sections of the country, there is considerably more latitude in correct wedding dress for men than for women. For example, a dark business or dress suit, a white shirt with tasteful tie, and black calf shoes are acceptable attire for the groom and groomsmen in many formal wedding situations before 6 P.M. Identical ties may be worn to provide added uniformity.

If you and the bride are undecided about what the men should wear, check with a consultant at a popular men's formal wear store in your community. He or she will be familiar with local customs and should be qualified to advise you.

Selecting Formal Wear

The following information may serve as a guide for grooms who are interested in the recommended formal wear for both daytime and nighttime weddings. Keep in mind that wedding styles for men do change or run in cycles. The suggested clothing may be rented at well equipped formal wear shops. Attendants from out of town may arrange to be measured at a rental wear store in their city and forward the information to the store you are using.

For very formal weddings after six, the groom and his attendants may wear formal clothing known as "white tie." This elegant traditional dress calls for black tailcoat and trousers with a white pique waistcoat, white shirt with wing collar, and white bow tie. Black patent or oxford shoes complete this sophisticated outfit along with black dress hose and white or pearl studs and cuff links.

For the very formal daytime wedding, the men may wear a black or oxford grey cutaway, grey and black striped trousers, grey waistcoat, and formal white shirt with a wing collar. Accessories may include a striped silk ascot with a pearl or gold stickpin, grey gloves, black shoes, and black socks.

For less formal weddings after six, the dress for men may vary with the season. From September to May, men may wear a tuxedo or formal dinner jacket with matching or coordinated trousers and vest. This outfit should be in black or subdued colors that coordinate. The shirt should be pleated or fancy bosom in white or colors with attached turndown collar. A black bow tie or one matching his shirt, vest or satin facings may be worn. For the less formal evening wedding from May to September, the man may choose a dinner jacket in white, pastels, vibrant colors, or patterns along with trousers that are black, matching, or coordinated with the coat. His vest may be matching or plain to coordinate. His shirt may be pleated or fancy bosom in white or colors with attached turndown collar. He should choose a black bow tie or one that matches his shirt or vest. Patent or polished calf shoes should be worn.

For the less formal daytime wedding, the man may wear the tuxedo of his choice or the classic stroller in granite grey or cafe brown. Trousers should be matching, coordinating, or classic stripe with a matching or coordinated vest. The shirt may be plain or fancy, in white or colors, with wing or attached turndown collar. A color-coordinated bow, striped ascot, or four-in-hand tie may be worn along with polished calf dress shoes.

Fathers' Dress

As a member of the wedding party, the bride's father usually dresses similar to the groomsmen. The groom's father has traditionally dressed as a guest. Today, however, practical considerations often call for the groom's father to dress the same as men in the wedding party. If he plans to take his place in the receiving line and at the bride's table, he will likely feel more comfortable if he is dressed similar to the bride's father. He will also look better in the wedding photographs if his attire harmonizes with that of the other men.

The Minister's Dress

It is appropriate for the minister to wear a robe or whatever he wears for normal pulpit dress. However, most clergymen will honor the wishes of the bride and groom if they want him to dress similar to other men in the wedding party.

Protecting Your Clothing

Unfortunately, many grooms must worry about things other than keeping their fiancée happy and selecting their wedding attire—such as protecting their clothing and shoes from misguided pranksters. One groom with rather large feet was greatly puzzled when the audience tittered as he knelt at the altar with his bride. With his back to the congregation, the soles of his shoes signaled the chalked message, "Help Me!" Another hapless groom discovered on his wedding night that the legs of his pajamas had been sewn together.

10
Entertaining and Being Entertained

The calendar of the weeks before the wedding will be filled with different social occasions. Many of the parties will center around the bride: a luncheon for members of the wedding party, kitchen or linen showers, or a morning coffee. Many of these events you will attend together as the guests of honor. At these functions, be sure to introduce groomsmen and members of your family to guests who do not know them.

The bride's parents may host an engagement party or friends or relatives may give a picnic or a patio party for you. Perhaps your mother or sisters will give a luncheon or a party to introduce the bride-to-be to their friends. This should not be a shower since the hostesses would be members of your immediate family.

There are some parties, however, that are strictly for the groom and his groomsmen and friends. A close friend or attendant may elect to give you the male equivalent of a shower. Groomsmen and friends through the years can get together to congratulate the groom and to bring items such as tools, toiletries, or outdoor cooking equipment. This party may be a patio buffet or cook-out.

Arranging the Bachelor Dinner

The bachelor dinner may be given by the groom as host or can be financed by the groomsmen with the best man doing most of the planning. Usually the dinner is held in a private room of a restaurant or club. If you are hosting the event, you should arrive early to put the gifts for your attendants in place and to greet your guests. Early in the evening the groom rises and proposes a toast to his bride. All the glasses are then tossed against a fireplace or wall, breaking them so they can never be used for a lesser purpose. As an alternative, the stems of the glasses may be snapped in two with the fingers. (The management can provide inexpensive stemware for this occasion.) Be sure to invite the two fathers to the bachelor dinner.

Sometimes it is impractical to try to give a bachelor dinner. The groomsmen from out of town may arrive just in time for the rehearsal the day before the wedding. The groom may not feel he can afford to give a dinner in a good restaurant.

Here are several alternatives to the bachelor party for gathering friends together and showing appreciation. A chili supper or carry-out pizza dinner at the groom's apartment would be fine. The day of the wedding, the groom may choose to entertain his attendants at a breakfast or brunch at a local restaurant.

The main entertaining responsibility of the groom and his family is the rehearsal dinner. This event is discussed in Chapter 15.

Finding Accommodations

The groom and his family are responsible for finding accommodations for all men and their wives in the wedding party. Sometimes relatives or family friends have an extra room they can provide for a groomsman. However, it may be necessary to secure rooms at a local motel or hotel. Check well in advance to get the best prices possible on a block of rooms. Note the proximity to the church and the reception site.

You will probably be asked to make a considerable down payment to hold the rooms. Your men will need to give you their dates of arrival and departure. Look the rooms over to be sure they are attractive and have the necessary amenities. A swimming pool and a nearby coffee shop are things that would add some pleasure and convenience to the stay.

Perhaps out-of-town guests who will not be attending the rehearsal dinner could be invited to drop by a friend's or relative's home where sandwiches and snacks would be provided. In this way friends have a chance to get together and feel a part of the festivities.

One groom who was being married away from home found a restored turn-of-the-century hotel with spacious verandas a few miles outside of Shelbyville, Tennessee, where the wedding was to be held. The Walking Horse Hotel served as headquarters for the groom's family and his groomsmen during the weekend of the wedding. The men enjoyed the player piano in the lobby, chats in the rocking chairs, walks in the quaint village, and memorabilia of champion walking horses.

The rustic hotel was also the scene of the rehearsal dinner on the evening before the ceremony and a hearty country brunch for the groomsmen and close friends on the morning of the wedding.

11
Selecting Flowers

Flowers for the ceremony set the stage for a lovely wedding. The bride will spend many hours visiting florists, describing in detail the mood she wishes to create, bearing in mind the cost and availability of the flowers. Her mother and her maid-of-honor may go with her to observe and help her compare options. The choices of decorating the church and reception hall and providing the bouquets for the bridal attendants are in the domain of the bride.

Nowadays the groom usually shares the financial responsibility for the flowers. Normally he pays for the bridal bouquet, corsages for the two mothers and possibly the grandmothers, and the boutonnieres for the groomsmen and other male members of the wedding party. If the groom lives out of town or is away at school, the bride and her mother may take care of choosing these flowers with a separate bill being sent to the groom from the flower shop. More informally, the groom may ask what his share of the costs are and pay the bride's parents.

Choosing the Bridal Bouquet

Since the groom provides the bride's bouquet, it might be fun for the two of you to go to the florist to select the flowers. Some brides still prefer the traditional white bouquet, but more than half now choose some color reflecting the bridesmaids' hues or the season of the year. Your fiancée will have definite ideas about a bouquet that will harmonize with her height, dress style, and fabric.

You may also order a corsage for your bride to wear as you leave the reception for the wedding trip. It is possible to arrange for a corsage to be incorporated into the bridal bouquet to be slipped out and pinned on the bride's "going away" suit. Incidentally, you or your best man may arrange for flowers to be in place in the hotel room when you arrive for your honeymoon.

Ordering Boutonnieres

At this time, you can order boutonnieres for the left lapel for yourself, the groomsmen, the two fathers, the minister, and the male musicians. Usually the flower for the groomsmen is a lily of the valley or a white carnation. The carnation may be dyed to match or to complement the color of the bridesmaids' gowns. The groom and the best man may wear a white rose or a flower that matches one in the bridal bouquet.

Choosing Corsages for the Mothers

Corsages for the mothers should harmonize with their gowns. Take into account their personal preferences in flowers as well as their heights and styles of dress. Also since these corsages may be worn during a lengthy reception, get advice on flowers that will look fresh for a long time.

A sentimental touch is to leave cards with the florist to enclose with the bridal bouquet and the mothers' flowers. A few words of love and appreciation to be read when they receive their flowers will endear you to these important women in your life.

While on the subject of flowers, why not bring a bouquet to your wife on the first payday after the honeymoon? These flowers need not be long-stemmed roses. Often the floral sections of super markets have lovely selections of cut flowers. You'll be off to a great start in keeping romance alive in your marriage.

12
Giving and Receiving Gifts

Most of the presents received by you and the bride will be items to grace your home or for day-to-day housekeeping. A groom may feel this is his fiancée's department and tend to leave choosing patterns for china, crystal, and silverware to her.

Visiting the Gift Registry

If you will spend an evening with your bride-to-be looking through brochures and leaflets, you will get an idea of what an exciting but quite confusing array of choices there are in fine things for the table. The two of you can then schedule a visit to a department store to settle on the patterns that you will be using for entertaining the rest of your lives.

The bride will surely appreciate her fiancé showing an interest and expressing some preferences. You and your fianceé could inquire about an open stock pattern that hopefully will be available for years to come. You could weigh the advantages of silver, silverplate, or the beautiful but sturdy stainless steel flatware used much today. If you have definite input into the choices, you can feel anticipation in using the lovely gifts.

The bride will register at a local store and probably a store in your home town for the convenience of your guests. In addition to registering the classic gifts of china, crystal, and silver, many stores encourage the listing of linens, small appliances, cooking utensils, and other accessories.

Receiving Gifts

Most of the gifts will be sent to the bride's home or to her parents. No doubt she has worked out a foolproof system of numbering and recording the presents with a notation as letters of acknowledgment are written.

Some gifts may be sent to you or your parents or handed to you by friends at work, school, or church. Many grooms take these gifts on to the bride so they may have the pleasure of opening them together. Be careful that all gifts given to you are noted and recorded in the bride's notebook.

As you look over the gifts on display at the bride's home, take special note of things given by your relatives or friends. Keep your parents informed so they can add a personal word of thanks to neighbors, friends, and co-workers.

Perhaps your attendants and friends will surprise you with a patio buffet or barbecue with you as the honored guest. One groom was "showered" with tools, socks, toiletries, cooking equipment, and handsome stationery. In such a case, a personal note to each of the friends is in order.

Writing Thank-You Notes

Your bride is probably doing her best to keep up with writing thank-you notes as gifts arrive. Doubtless there will still be plenty to write after returning from the honeymoon. She will try to have them finished within a couple of months after the wedding trip. If she is writing to a friend of yours whom she does not know, you might write two or three sentences on the note after she has penned the first line or two. Remember, it is a big responsibility for the bride to get all acknowledgments on the way within a reasonable length of time. Don't feel neglected if she seems to be spending most of her spare time with pen in hand.

Selecting the Bride's Gift

You may consider the honeymoon as your gift to the bride. You may choose to give a tangible gift also—something that will be treasured for years to come. This gift may be jewelry, such as a pearl necklace, a gold bracelet, a dinner ring, or perhaps a watch. A leather briefcase she could carry to work or a new tennis racquet for the honeymoon are different and welcome ideas. Another possibility that would delight a bride is a family heirloom in jewelry or something for the house. For example, a great-grandmother's lavaliere or silver sugar and cream set or a pair of silver candlesticks would thrill your new bride and make her feel a cherished member of the family.

Choosing Gifts for Groomsmen

Gifts to the best man and the groomsmen are usually something that can be worn in the wedding or that can be engraved with a monogram and the date of the wedding. One groom gave each of his attendants a silk tie the shade of the bridesmaids' dresses. Worn during the ceremony, these ties helped coordinate the attire of the wedding party.

Cuff links, money clips, tie pins, revere bowls, and pewter mugs are popular choices. These gifts can be a lasting remembrance of your wedding day. Also you might choose useful gifts such as luggage, a special golf club, a leather wallet, or a fine writing pen, perhaps selecting different gifts for each attendant. However, gifts for the groomsmen should be of approximately the same value, while the gift for the best man may be somewhat more expensive. You may present these gifts at the bachelor dinner or the rehearsal dinner.

13
Packing and Wardrobe Planning

It's a good idea to start thinking about your day-to-day wardrobe at least a few weeks before you start packing for your wedding trip. This is a good time to go through your clothing and discard garments that are badly worn or that you no longer wear.

It's particularly important to throw away tattered underwear and pajamas. Your bride will appreciate attractive underclothing as well as outer garments.

You may need to buy new clothing if your budget will allow. Most clothing experts say that it's better to have a limited number of good basic garments—suits, slacks, sports coats, and blazers—than a large quantity of clothing.

The intelligent man will choose clothing that fits his lifestyle and that may be layered according to weather conditions. Using sweaters, boots, shirts and ties judiciously, you can easily dress "up" or dress "down" as the occasion demands.

The "natural" tones such as beige or grey are easier to match and coordinate than bright or fad colors. Many men like the good looks and versatility of the camel's hair or navy blazer in wool or wool blend.

If you're going to a tropical location for your honeymoon, you'll find lightweight white or pastel clothing comfortable and stylish. You should also remember to take a raincoat.

Most inexperienced travelers are tempted to take too many clothes on a trip because it is easier to take everything in sight than it is to make advance decisions about what you'll need. Incidentally, if the honeymoon location is supposed to be a big secret even to your bride, at least tell her what kind of climate to expect so that she can bring appropriate clothing.

You'll want to choose a few basic garments for normal weather conditions plus one or two sweaters or jackets you can add or remove as comfort dictates. If most of your time will be spent on the beach or in your hotel room, perhaps you'll need only one or two dress-up outfits. Try to get by with a couple of pairs of shoes. It's doubly important that you travel light if you're going by plane or train.

Before starting to pack, write out a list of clothing and accessories you plan to take. Lay everything out on the bed before you begin packing. Everything should be clean and well pressed. Trousers, shirts and blazers should be packed first if these larger items are not being carried in a garment bag.

Roll jeans, tee shirts, sweaters and pajamas to conserve space. Socks, handkerchiefs, and underwear may be used to stuff shoes, fill spaces, and form cushions around fragile items such as a hair dryer. Tuck ties, belts, socks and underwear around the edges. Pack your toiletries separately in a shaving kit (trial size bottles are ideal).

Any wrinkles should disappear after your clothes are unpacked and placed on hangers. Hanging them in a damp area such as a bathroom will cause the wrinkles to disappear. Take along a plastic bag for your laundry.

If your luggage is looking worn or shabby, this is a good time to replace it. Quality luggage is an investment that should last for years. Select luggage that is part of a set and then add pieces as you need them. Look for convenience features such as locks and shoulder straps. Shop for a classic style and color that you won't tire of in a year or two. Check construction and durability. Be sure closures work smoothly and that the fabric wears well. You'll also want your luggage to lift and handle well. Many stores discount luggage considerably at certain seasons of the year. If you're going to need luggage, start looking early and find yourself a terrific buy.

14
Preserving the Memories

The wedding itself will last only about a half hour. But the occasion is the culmination of weeks of planning and may well be the biggest event in your lives. Everything that is practical should be done to preserve these memories.

This special day can be best preserved by good wedding photography and a quality sound recording of the ceremony. A printed program will also serve as a cherished souvenir for the wedding party and all of the guests. A memory box containing mementos of wedding activities will become increasingly precious to the bride and you over the years. With the growing popularity of home videotape recorders, it is now possible in most cities to have the wedding videotaped for replay on your television set.

Photographing the Wedding

Before the bride chooses a photographer, it's a good idea to check with the church to learn about any restrictions on wedding pictures. For example, many churches will not permit flash photography during the ceremony and pictures of the actual ceremony must be taken from a distance with available light. If a photographer is selected who is not familiar with the layout of the wedding site, he should visit the location before the ceremony.

Wedding photography is very demanding because the photographer will not have a second chance to capture these fleeting memories in living color. By all means an experienced wedding photographer should be chosen who knows what, when and how to document the wedding. Such photographers are in heavy demand, particularly during the peak wedding season, so you and the bride will want to engage your photographer as soon as possible.

Since your fianceé will likely need your assistance in arranging for memorable pictures, here are some suggestions. First, check with friends who have had satisfactory experience with a wedding photographer, including delivery of the initial pictures within two or three weeks. We have known brides who waited months before their wedding pictures were delivered.

If you're not familiar with a photographer's work, take a close look at his wedding portfolio. Be specific about what you want and get a firm price. You may be able to negotiate for a price if he does not offer a package deal you like.

Most photographers will offer two or three "packages" which include a good number of small (or proof) prints plus a selection of enlargements. Additional pictures may be ordered at a specified cost. You can also arrange for the photographer to take a color portrait of the bride along with black and white pictures for the engagement announcement at the final fitting of her bridal gown. The photographer will probably want a partial payment (up to 50 percent) on the wedding day with the balance due when the pictures are delivered.

Most brides want a good selection of both formal (or posed) pictures and candid shots. This arrangement will require the photographer to spend two hours or more at the wedding site when the reception follows at the same location. He will need to arrive at the church or hall at least an hour before the ceremony to set up his equipment and take such pictures as the bride's mother adjusting the bride's veil, the bridesmaids completing their preparations, the groom and the best man in waiting, and the bride and her father arriving at the church or emerging from the dressing room.

After the ceremony, the photographer's objective should be to get the necessary pictures without inconveniencing the guests who want to greet the bride and groom. It is inexcusable to have guests waiting in line for half an hour or more before they can be admitted to the reception area.

Most professional photographers can get the required post-ceremony pictures in about twenty minutes. A good procedure is to take the large group pictures first and release the people who will not be needed any more. This arrangement will permit most members of the wedding party and close relatives to mingle with the guests while the bride and groom are completing the photographs.

After the auditorium pictures are completed, the photographer will want to take photos of the receiving line and informal shots of the family and guests. Traditional pictures, such as throwing the bridal bouquet may be taken, along with pictures of guests throwing rice as the couple departs. If the bride and groom change to travel clothes before leaving, this memory should be photographed.

In addition to the pictures ordered by the bride and her parents, you'll want to provide an album of pictures for your parents. An album with 5 x 5 or 5 x 7 prints is a handy size to carry as well as to display on a coffee table. It's also a nice gesture to provide small pictures of the wedding party for each of your attendants and close relatives.

Friends who enjoy taking pictures should be encouraged to take candid shots at the wedding and the reception. These informal photos will complement the more formal pictures taken by the professional photographer.

Recording the Ceremony

A sound recording of the wedding will provide a cherished memory of the ceremony at very small cost. If the church or club where the wedding is to be held can make the recording through its sound system, you will likely get better results. Some churches provide this service on cassette tapes for less than $20. Additional copies can be made for a few dollars each.

If the church or hall cannot make the recording for you, ask for their permission to tape the ceremony. One or more microphones will need to be placed as close to the altar as possible, preferably attached to the public address microphone. If no public address system is to be used, a microphone could be placed in the flowers. A small recorder can be hidden behind the flowers.

Preparing a Printed Program

A printed program of the service will assist your guests in following the ceremony, identifying the music and members of the wedding party, and providing a treasured souvenir for everyone who attends. If the wedding is being held at a church, it is possible that the church office will assist in preparing the program on its equipment at modest cost.

The simplest format other than an unfolded sheet is the 4¼ x 5½ folder resulting from one fold of an 8½ x 11 sheet. The original can be prepared by any good typist for reproduction. One bride's mother who is gifted in calligraphy prepared a distinctive program by hand. The program was beautifully reproduced by offset printing on a textured ivory paper matching the bridal colors.

Videotaping the Wedding

If you or the bride have access to a video cassette recorder, you may want to consider videotaping the wedding service and the reception for projection on your home television set. This service is surprisingly reasonable in some large cities, but be sure to view the firm's work before making a commitment. The degree of professionalism varies considerably. Most videotape services can produce tape for playback on either the Beta or VHS format recorders.

15
Planning the Rehearsal Dinner

The rehearsal dinner or party is customarily given by the groom's family but may properly be given by the bride's family, a friend or a relative. We recommend that the groom's family host this occasion whenever feasible, particularly if the bride's parents are giving a reception for all wedding guests.

This dinner, normally held immediately before or after the ceremony rehearsal, offers the groom and his parents the best opportunity to entertain the wedding party and others closely associated with the bride and groom. This occasion may also be the means of the groom's family assuming the responsibility and expense of a major wedding event in a pleasant, positive way.

If your family wants to give the rehearsal party or dinner, tell your bride-to-be. You and your parents should then coordinate the plans with the rehearsal schedule. The occasion may, of course, be as casual or as lavish as your taste and budget allows.

The dinner is most frequently held immediately after the ceremony rehearsal, usually on the evening before the wedding. The dinner should be attended by all members of the wedding party and their spouses or fiancés, and, of course, both sets of parents, grandparents, and other members of the immediate family. Be sure to invite the minister and his wife and perhaps the wedding musicians.

Close friends of the hostess and out-of-town guests who have arrived for the wedding may also be invited. Ask the bride's mother to prepare a list of people she would like to invite to be sure no one is overlooked. Your parents will probably request that persons invited "R.S.V.P." by a given date for the caterer's information.

Selecting a Place

It is ideal if the dinner is held near the rehearsal site to avoid wasted motion and the possibility of someone's getting lost. (You may want to enclose a simple map with the dinner invitation if you feel that guests may have difficulty in locating the site.) Possible locations are a hotel or club, a popular restaurant, your home, or the church building. You and your parents should select a place in keeping with your budget that will accommodate your guests comfortably. Other important considerations are the atmosphere and the service you desire. You might get ideas from other families who have recently had successful rehearsal dinners.

If you prefer a casual rehearsal party, an informal buffet in someone's home can be just as enjoyable as—and less expensive than — a formal dinner at a club or restaurant. For maximum convenience, the hostess at the church where the wedding is being held may be able to cater the dinner.

Choosing a Caterer

If you decide to use a hotel, club, or restaurant, make reservations as early as possible. Many popular catering halls are booked months in advance. You may want to look at several places before making a decision. Check out the facilities and compare menus. Ask for a guaranteed price. Don't sign anything until you find what you want.

The rehearsal dinner should be a festive occasion, including toasts to the future happiness of the bride and groom. The best man should begin the toasting and usually acts as emcee for the occasion.

Planning the Program

The best man will likely need your help in planning an entertaining program—but you can expect him to reserve a surprise or two for you and the bride. Many of the people dearest to you and the bride will reflect on the good times you have had together. Some of these expressions from your friends and relatives may be touching, hilarious—or even embarrassing!

One resourceful best man arranged a "memory box dowry" each for the bride and the groom for presentation to the spouse-to-be at the rehearsal dinner. With confidential help from family members, items were assembled such as the bride's first Barbie doll and elementary school diary, and the groom's first Hot Wheels and baseball glove. The matron of honor and other friends assisted the best man in presenting each item from the "memory box" to the delight of the couple and the guests.

Perhaps the hotel or restaurant will provide flowers or other decorations for the tables if you request them. Otherwise, your mother and her friends will need to assume this responsibility.

Because of the relative intimacy of the rehearsal dinner, seating need not be as structured as it might be at a larger formal reception. Many hostesses prefer a seating arrangement that encourages fellowship and compatibility. A family member or close friend may be asked to serve as an informal host at each table.

Rather than using place cards, you may prefer to simply assign guests to a table, allowing them to choose their seats. If place cards are used, have them prepared by someone who has some skill in hand lettering or calligraphy.

Music before and during dinner by a pianist, organist, or other musicians will enhance the festivities. Ask your musician to play a combination of current hits and old favorites, including songs you and the bride particularly like.

If neither you nor your parents lives in the city where you are being married, it may be necessary for the bride's family to make arrangements for the dinner. In this instance, your family will still host the event, and, of course, pay the bill.

16
Rehearsing Your Wedding

Your fiancée or her mother is responsible for working out a time to rehearse the wedding with the minister or other officiant. The rehearsal is usually held on the night before the ceremony. The rehearsal dinner, customarily given by the groom's family, is normally scheduled immediately before or after the wedding rehearsal.

The bride's mother or a wedding director designated by her normally takes charge of the rehearsal with assistance from the presiding minister. This run-through is most important because it is the final opportunity to work out procedures and iron out any problems before the wedding.

You and your best man can contribute to a good rehearsal by seeing that all men in the wedding party are on time for the rehearsal and pay close attention to what goes on. If any one of your men is absolutely unable to attend, appoint one of your groomsmen to note his cues and positions and have him practice it privately with the attendant before the ceremony.

The ushers will need to be briefed on the procedures for seating guests and carrying out special duties such as lighting the candles or spreading the aisle carpet. The men designated to seat the mothers should be prepared to do this easily.

Your bride-to-be may prefer to use a stand-in rather than rehearsing the vows and standing at the altar with you. You can bet that she is paying close attention to what is going on and will proudly take her place at your side for the actual event.

If your parents are hosting a dinner immediately after the rehearsal, they will likely need to leave the rehearsal before it is concluded. Unless your father is in the wedding party, your parents' main concern at the rehearsal will be their cues for being ushered to and from their seats.

One final thought: don't be too upset if the rehearsal seems to be hectic or slightly disorganized. Most ceremony run throughs with several attendants require a good bit of trial and error before final procedures are adopted. The main concern is for all questions to be cleared up before the wedding party leaves the rehearsal. Chances are very good that everything will flow smoothly when the "real thing" gets underway.

17
Enjoying the Wedding Day

Your wedding day is one of the great days of your life. Although some anxiety is natural, you owe it to yourself and to your fiancée to enjoy your special day as much as possible. Careful planning with attention to important details will help things run smoothly for everyone.

First, resist the temptation to do too much celebrating the night before your wedding—whether with your bride or with the boys. You'll benefit from a good night's sleep.

Calling Your Bride

You may want to observe the tradition of not seeing your bride on the wedding day until you meet her at the altar. She'll particularly not want you to see her in her wedding gown before the ceremony. You should, however, call your fiancée on the morning of the wedding and reassure her that you are as enthusiastic—and perhaps as nervous—about the ceremony as she is.

If you're at home with your parents, be considerate of them on your big day. Use your groomsmen or, better still, relatives not involved in the wedding for any last-minute services or errands.

Conferring with Your Best Man

You'll likely want to confer with your best man early in the day—perhaps at a relaxing breakfast. If you've selected an efficient and composed best man, the two of you can make certain that everything is in readiness. The groom's checklist on page 75 may be used for this purpose.

You'll need to know that all of your attendants are in town with everything they need. At a wedding being held out of town, one of the ushers realized on the night before the ceremony that he had forgotten to pick up his wedding clothing. Fortunately, another usher was returning to the city that night and was able to bring the tuxedo the next day.

Make certain that you have the marriage license and give it to the best man for completion by the officiant. Deliver the wedding ring to the best man to be handed back to you at the appointed time in the ceremony. You'll also give him the minister's fee in an envelope for presentation just before or after the ceremony. (You may use cash or a check made out to the minister).

How much should the honorarium be, since most ministers have no set fee? Practices vary considerably from place to place, depending on the size of the wedding, the amount of time given by the minister, and local customs. There should be additional compensation for out-of-town travel or other unusual expenses.

You'll want to make sure that your going-away car is in good condition. If you've not finished packing, ask your best man to help you. Turn the luggage, reservations, and other important papers over to him for safekeeping. He'll also see that your fiancée's luggage is added to yours.

If your wedding is scheduled for late afternoon or evening, you might enjoy an informal brunch or early lunch with your groomsmen. This could be a particularly convenient and pleasant diversion if all of you are away from home and staying at the same place. It's also a good time to make certain everything is in order for the men. You might also deliver the gifts for your attendants. Be sure to include the bride's father and your own father.

It's your best man's duty to get you to the church on time and help you dress. If the two of you will dress at home or at the hotel, you should arrive at the church an hour before the ceremony. You'll need an hour and a half if you are dressing at the church. It's important that you feel relaxed and unhurried.

Once you are dressed for the wedding, you'll have your boutonniere pinned on you and probably be photographed with the best man. The two of you will meet the minister at the designated time and place. Your mother and father will be seated five minutes before the ceremony. The bride's mother will be escorted to her seat immediately after your parents are seated. The wedding drama has officially begun!

Surviving the Ceremony

At the first strains of the processional, you and your best man follow the minister into the church from a side door and take your positions at the altar. You watch and wait expectantly as the groomsmen and bridesmaids enter and take their positions on either side.

As the processional reaches its climax, your bride enters on her father's arm. She is breathtakingly beautiful! You smile as she joins you at the first pew or perhaps at the altar. The solemn and sacred ceremony then proceeds as you have rehearsed it. Here's some advice from a recent bride, "Tell the groom to look at his bride rather than at the minister when he says his vows."

When the ceremony is over and the minister has congratulated the two of you, the bride's face veil, if one is used, is lifted for the traditional kiss (optional).

Upon the organist's signal, the bride will take your arm and you will start up the aisle together. The bride's attendants quickly fall into step behind her. The honor attendant is on the right arm of the best man and each bridesmaid is on the arm of an usher. Extra ushers walk together at the end. On reaching the vestibule, the ushers previously designated return to escort the mothers and honored guests from the church. You and the bride, along with other members of the wedding party, will return immediately to the sanctuary for photographs. Your guests will be directed to the reception site.

Greeting Friends at the Reception

You and the bride may take your place in a formal receiving line, or you may prefer to greet your guests informally. In the latter case, you and your bride will want to circulate among the guests throughout the evening. It is, of course, easier to move from guest to guest if you are having a stand-up reception rather than a seated dinner.

If a receiving line is used, you'll take your place with the bride along with her mother, your parents, and the maid of honor. The participation of the bride's father and the bridesmaids is optional. The best man and the ushers do not stand in the receiving line.

You'll introduce your bride to friends she may not know and say "thank you" to congratulations and good wishes. As much as you'd like to chat with friends at this time, it's best not to introduce subjects that might prolong the greeting and hold up the line.

When the guests have all been greeted, you'll take your bride to the bridal table for dinner or whatever food has been provided. You'll stand with her on your right, your hand over hers on the knife, when she cuts the wedding cake. You'll respond graciously when your best man proposes a toast to you and the bride.

Perhaps there was a time when the bride and groom left the reception early to get away on their wedding trip. Nowadays, the couple is more likely to linger with their friends—some of whom have come long distances to be with them. Most receptions tend to break up shortly after the newly married couple leaves. So take your time and enjoy your friends, even though you and your beloved are eager to be alone.

Before the festivities end, it is customary for the bride to throw her bouquet among the bridesmaids and other unmarried guests. Either you or the bride may toss her garter to a throng of single men.

Saying Good-bye

Arrange for a time when you can say good-bye to the bride's parents and your parents before the mad dash to the car for the wedding trip. Perhaps a good time to do this would be just before or after you change clothes. You'll also want to shake hands with your attendants before you receive a shower of rice.

Depend on your best man to see that your luggage and that of your bride is packed in your car or shipped ahead to your destination. You should arrange for him to take care of your car and your important papers until you're dressed and ready to leave on your honeymoon. He will also accompany you as you leave the reception and may drive you off if you like.

You may want the best man to send a telegram in your name to your new in-laws thanking them for the beautiful wedding. The best man, or another dependable person, should be responsible for returning all rental clothing to the store.

18
Arranging a Memorable Honeymoon

The object of a honeymoon is to get to know each other better in relaxed surroundings that are free of distractions. A young groom in England missed the point altogether. He sent his twenty-one-year-old bride off with his mother on a five-day visit to a Channel Island resort while he remained at home to run his store.

The bride admitted she missed him like mad even though she got along very well with his mother, and they had a lovely time. The groom's philosophy was, "In my book, business comes first. If you can't make money, you can't live."

Assuming you are a groom who prefers companionship to commerce after your wedding, you must plan carefully all details of the honeymoon, arranging reservations, passports, and needed insurance in advance. The honeymoon must be planned as carefully as the wedding.

You will want to keep travel time after the ceremony rather short to avoid fatigue. This may mean that you will need at least one overnight stop before you reach your destination. Your bride will appreciate your thoughtfulness if you (or the best man) arrange for flowers to be in your room when you arrive. You'll perhaps enjoy having dinner for two served in your room the first evening.

Let the hotel or airline know you will be newlyweds, as many include special services for just-married couples. One young groom on a budget inquired about the honeymoon suite at a popular hotel for the first night of the wedding trip. After the rate was quoted, he opted for a regular room. Upon arriving at the hotel, to his surprise and delight, he had been given the honeymoon suite for the cost of a standard room.

Deciding Where to Go

Many people associate the honeymoon with an extravagant trip to the Caribbean, staying in a fine hotel and dining at posh restaurants. Imagine this—sun-filled days on the beach, water skiing and sailing, followed by tennis on a manicured court. Then after a siesta, there is a bike tour of historic places on the island. For supper, how about seafood cooked local style! In the Caribbean, that could be Dutch, French, Spanish, or British depending on your island. After watching a spectacular and romantic moonrise, choose for the evening authentic folk entertainment or perhaps stroll on the beach and listen to the sounds of the sea.

If your wedding takes place between mid-April and mid-December, the Caribbean offers discounts of 25 to 50 percent on hotel bills and many other special prices.

A dream honeymoon for you and your bride might be a tour of Europe—the first trip abroad for each of you. What a grand memory to share of your first days together as man and wife. A sightseeing honeymoon does have its drawbacks, however. You may feel guilty for not taking advantage of every opportunity to visit a museum or tour a place of interest. A highly structured ten days with every hour crammed with exciting things to do and see may seem too much of a good thing when you would prefer to spend the afternoon at the pool.

One couple carried their tennis racquets along on their honeymoon with plans to play tennis every day—but ended up not playing at all. They found they were physically and emotionally exhausted after the wedding with its crowded calendar of social events, and then some tiring travel to the honeymoon site.

The Pennsylvania Pocono Mountains are traditional for a glamourous honeymoon without leaving the country. Here you can ski on a playground of snow in the winter or water ski on a crystal lake during the warm season. Through the years, innkeepers of the Poconos have learned to cater to bridal couples in a personal but unobtrusive manner. The hotels might offer a private villa for the bride and groom featuring a log-burning fireplace, a heart-shaped bath, a Jacuzzi all their own, and a balcony overlooking a lake. Also there is gourmet dining, nightly entertainment, and, for fellowship, a midnight buffet. Sports include snowmobiling, archery, tobagganing, swimming in a heated pool, and, of course, hikes through the forest.

The Poconos' vacations are packaged so that one price includes lodging, meals, and recreational facilities as well as entertainment each evening. You will know how much you will pay and will not be in danger of running short of money the last couple of days of your wedding trip.

Perhaps you and your fiancée share a hobby: skiing, painting, fishing, antiques, or gourmet food. It would be fun to keep these interests in mind as you plan a fun-filled time in Colorado, New England, or New Orleans.

Consult your local travel agent. Tell him how much you want to spend, how long you'll be traveling, and your general interests. He'll have some great ideas and his service is free.

After you've chosen the area you want to visit, you can write the Chamber of Commerce or tourist bureau and inquire about local rentals. You may discover a cozy beach house or mountain cabin that rents far below the cottages or condos your agent would know about.

Planning When Time Or Money Is Short

Extravagant honeymoons cost a lot of money. Even if the travel and hotel costs are kept down through a package deal, food, tips, and night life can add up. Chances are there is a resort area in your own state which you have not visited. Many state parks offer truly outstanding lodges, restaurants, and recreation at very moderate prices, and too these parks are usually located in areas of scenic beauty. You could save time and money.

One couple, who had both been working hard at responsible jobs while planning their wedding in the bride's hometown five hundred miles away, wanted a change of pace for the wedding trip. A comfortable, quiet cabin on a South Carolina beach suited them fine. They enjoyed the treat of fresh seafood prepared in their own kitchenette. Beach games, walks along the shore, and lazy afternoons filled most of their days. A day in historic Charleston gave them a chance for some sightseeing and dinner at an elegant restaurant.

Perhaps relatives or friends have a vacation cottage you could use free or at a slight cost. What about borrowing or renting a camper or a recreational vehicle? An examiniation of the classified ad page may turn up a low-cost rental condo in a resort area or near a lake.

If only a weekend can be allotted for the honeymoon, look into some of the three-day specials offered at the better hotels in your area. Enjoy a cut-rate price on a nice room, Sunday brunch, evening entertainment, and other amenities of a luxury hotel.

If time is extremely short the most practical thing might be to defer the honeymoon and spend the weekend in your new apartment, provided things are reasonably in place. Take time out for a meal in a posh restaurant. Make plans as soon as possible to have the honeymoon of your dreams.

Tipping Suggestions

Here are a few ideas on tipping. You will be coming in contact with a number of people who are normally given gratuities for their services. A good rule is to tip fifteen percent for good service.

If you plan to stay in a hotel more than a night or two, tip the chambermaid fifty cents to a dollar a night. Note whether a restaurant bill includes a gratuity. Bellhop service is at least fifty cents per bag. The hat check girl gets fifty cents also. A tip to the maitre d' at the beginning of your stay at a resort hotel will assure you courteous, attentive service.

Taking Pictures of the Wedding Trip

Be sure to take your camera and extra film along on the honeymoon. Create a pictorial record of your honeymoon from start to finish. Have your best man snap you and your bride as you pack the car. Be sure the "Just Married" decorations show. Get someone to take a photo of you two together, standing in front of the hotel (with its name in view) or making castles in the sand.

Take pictures of the natives—the Cajuns of Louisiana or the fishermen of the Caribbean. Get a picture of the couple you enjoyed spending time with. Take some mailers along so you can send the film to the processors as soon as it is exposed. Maybe some snapshots of your honeymoon will be waiting for you when you return home.

While you will have thoughts only of each other for the first couple of days, you and the bride will want to call your families while you are away. They will be delighted to hear from you, and you can tell them again how much the wedding meant to you. They will also appreciate picture postcards with the flavor of your honeymoon paradise.

19
Paying the Bills

You'll enjoy your wedding a great deal more if you know precisely what your financial obligations are. Be prepared to pay your bills promptly. Careful planning and budgeting will be required to achieve this.

As pointed out in the Preface, the wedding expenses of the groom and his parents may actually exceed those of the bride's family if the cost of an engagement ring is added along with other costly items such as the honeymoon and a rehearsal dinner. If the wedding is held outside your home town, you will likely have additional expenses for food, lodging, and transportation.

Deciding Who Pays for What

In order for you and your family to get a complete picture of wedding costs, the following list covers the traditional obligations of all parties concerned. Keep in mind that you and your bride may not require all of these items for your wedding. You may, of course, need others that are not listed. More important than who pays for a given item is the fact that the two families have freely discussed the expenses and reached a satisfactory agreement.

The bride or her parents pay for:
Wedding invitations and announcements
Bridal gown and accessories

Flowers for the wedding and the reception
Fees for soloist, organist, and custodian
The entire reception (cake, food, drink, musicians)
Rental of church building or hall
Photography, recordings, etc.
Groom's wedding band
Gifts for bridesmaids
Gift for the groom
Lodging for out-of-town bridal attendants
Transportation for the bridal party

The groom or his parents are responsible for:
The bride's engagement ring and wedding band
Gift for the bride
The bridal bouquet and boutonnieres for attendants
Flowers for the mothers
Wedding clothes for the groom
Wedding clothes for the groom's parents
Gifts for the ushers and best man
Bachelor dinner
Rehearsal dinner
Accommodations for groom's attendants
Marriage license
Minister's honorarium (fee)
The honeymoon

The attendants are responsible for:
Their clothing for the wedding
Any travel expenses if from out of town (lodging is provided)
Wedding gift

Saving Money (Without Cutting Quality)

As you and your bride plan the wedding, be realistic about what you are able to spend. You'll need to speak up right away if you and your parents are going to have difficulty handling your part of the expenses. Perhaps the festivities could be scaled down before elaborate arrangements are made. Suggestions have been made in previous chapters about cost-cutting. Several of these suggestions are repeated here for convenience.

If you can't afford to buy the engagement ring you'd like to give, you might consider giving her a birthstone or other semi-precious stone with the understanding that you'll give her a diamond when your financial situation improves. If you know a diamond broker or manufacturing jeweler, he may be able to save you money on a diamond. However, don't take chances on a dealer who is not well established.

Are you having a daytime wedding or a not-so-formal evening wedding? You could talk with your fiancée about you and your attendants wearing appropriate dark business suits that are already in your wardrobes rather than renting formal clothes.

Identical four-in-hand ties can be purchased by the attendants to provide some uniformity at relatively small cost. One groom presented tasteful silk ties to his groomsmen matching the bridesmaids' colors for the ceremony.

The rehearsal dinner, normally given by your parents, doesn't have to be held at the most plush hotel or club in town. Consider a buffet served at your parents' home or at the home of a friend. Perhaps the church where the wedding is to be held is equipped to serve a seated dinner that would be festive as well as convenient.

If you want to use a club or restaurant, look for a smaller restaurant that serves good food without charging more than you can afford. An out-of-the-way place with an interesting atmosphere may please your guests as much as the country club or an exclusive restaurant. Sometimes a new hotel will offer attractive food prices in order to build its clientele.

Lodging for your out-of-town attendants can be expensive. Perhaps close friends or relatives would consent for these members of the wedding party to stay in their homes. If you must accommodate several people, contact hotels and motels early and negotiate for the best rates.

The bachelor dinner, often given by the groom for his attendants, is said to be a dying institution. Perhaps the increasing popularity of a rehearsal dinner hosted by the groom's family leaves less time for the old "stag" dinner. In any case, you and your men can get together informally without expensive food and entertainment. If some of your friends want to sponsor the dinner, don't be too proud to accept their hospitality.

You, of course, want to shop carefully for the gifts you'll be presenting to your best man and ushers. If you allow yourself plenty of time to browse at boutiques and specialty shops, you may be able to find very appropriate gifts at attractive prices.

Possible savings on the honeymoon are suggested in the section entitled "Planning When Time Or Money Is Short" (page 63, Chapter 18). The principal thing is to decide what kind of wedding trip you and your bride would enjoy most. If such a honeymoon is not within your means, your options include the following:

(1) Shorten the wedding trip. A paid-up one week honeymoon may be better than two weeks on credit.
(2) Consider a similar setting nearer to home. It may not be Hawaii, but you can get there sooner and enjoy it longer.
(3) Choose less exotic lodging. Maybe you really don't have to have a Jacuzzi in your suite.
(4) Use your kitchen as much as practical. While you don't want meal preparation to be burdensome, make eating out something special. You might cook a couple of your specialties for her.
(5) Settle for less commercial entertainment. Try entertaining yourselves with long walks on the beach or hikes in the mountains; pack a picnic lunch and perhaps take in a local craft fair or folk festival.
(6) Use buses and shuttles rather than taxis. A honeymoon is no place for haste, anyway.

Your Wedding Budget

This budget form may be used by both you and your parents in planning for the wedding expenditures suggested in the previous section. You will need to adapt the form for your special circumstances.

Responsibilities of you and your parents:
Engagement ring   _____
Wedding band for bride   _____
Marriage license   _____
Gift for bride   _____
Gifts for best man and ushers   _____
Bachelor dinner   _____

Rehearsal dinner _____
Bridal bouquet and boutonnieres _____
Flowers for mothers _____
Wedding attire for groom _____
Wedding attire for parents _____
Lodging for attendants _____
Minister's honorarium (fee) _____
The honeymoon
   Travel expenses _____
   Food and lodging _____
   Entertainment _____
   Total for honeymoon ══════
Total Wedding Expenses for Groom and Parents ══════

20
Getting Settled

If you are moving into a new house or apartment, you'll want to arrange for all of the utilities to be operative by the time you move in. You'll find it frustrating if you return from the honeymoon and the heat (or air conditioning) is off and the telephone doesn't work.

Furnishing Your Home

Shortly before or after your honeymoon, you and your bride must preside over the "marriage" of your furniture and household goods. You'll need to discard worn out items. You'll also have to integrate the wedding gifts into the decor of your new home.

If you're entering a small apartment, you may have to store some things until you get more space. If you're fortunate enough to have more room than you need, you may not have enough furniture to supply all your rooms. In that case you may need to close one of the bedrooms or a formal living room in favor of a small den.

In furnishing your place, you may end up using your stereo, her bedroom suite, a dining set from her parents, and a sofa you bought together, and so on. Wedding gifts such as lamps, candle-sticks, and pictures can be skillfully used to "finish off" each of the rooms.

Chances are you'll receive a fine selection of kitchen wares and bedding. It is, of course, proper to return duplicate gifts or ones you can't use in exchange for things you need.

Managing Your Money

Good money management may seem simple enough: just be certain that you save a part of all that you make without going into debt more than your income justifies and pay your bills promptly. You and your bride will find, however, that you can't carry out these goals without careful planning, patience, and cooperation.

The fact that marriage is supposed to be an equal partnership sometimes makes it more difficult for you to keep up with your money. Neither of you may want to dictate priorities and the financial partnership may fail to function properly. The answer is good communication and enough organization to get the job done. You'll want to discuss your thoughts and feelings about financial matters openly and make basic decisions together.

Money managers advise young couples to write a financial plan. Such a plan could incude a household budget with four categories: Income, Emergency Fund, Living Expenses, and Savings Account. This plan calls for dividing your savings into two accounts for specified purposes.

The Emergency Fund is a savings program to provide protection in case of change of jobs, serious illness, etc. Most authorities agree that this amount should be equivalent to three to six months' take home pay. It will take strong discipline to avoid the temptation to use this money for purposes other than emergencies.

It's best to put all available money beyond living expenses into the Emergency Fund until it reaches the desired level. You should then open a second savings account for such things as vacations, taxes, education, and other special items such as investments. It's wise to get your Emergency Fund and Savings Account well established before making speculative investments.

You must give priority to your savings program if it is to grow. If you don't take out money for savings first of all, you may not do much saving. There will always be some good reason to skip savings if the two of you don't commit yourselves to it.

You should agree on a regular amount to deposit into your savings account each month. Then increase this amount when either of your gets a raise. Perhaps your employer offers a payroll savings plan with a bank or credit union that would make it easier for you to put something aside each payday.

How much should you save? This is for the two of you to decide. It's a matter of your goals and sense of values. How important is it to have things now as opposed to sacrificing a bit in order to have more tomorrow?

A significant decision for the two of you will be who makes the deposits, writes the checks, and balances the bank statement. Perhaps one of you has more time or interest to give to financial management than the other. It is most important that this be discussed and for both of you to agree on a plan. You may decide for one of you to make the transactions with the two of you reviewing them periodically. Most couples decide on a plan of sharing the duties.

If you adopt the sharing plan, we recommend two checking accounts with each partner specifically responsible for various payments. Otherwise, both of you will be writing checks out of the same account, and maintaining a current balance becomes more difficult. Incidentally, it will be easier to keep up with expenditures if you will pay everything by check or credit card except for money from your personal allowance.

Reach an agreement on financial procedure with your mate and do your best to stick to it. If your plan isn't working after a good try, the two of you should devise something else.

Controlling Your Credit

Credit is a way of life in today's society. It provides a convenient way for you to purchase items now for which you cannot afford full payment. A major advantage of credit is the ability to borrow for emergencies or to make major purchases such as a home or an automobile. Credit accounts also enable a person to take advantage of sales and other special buying opportunities.

The wide use of credit cards has given rise to the expression "plastic society." These charge cards are a useful means for paying your bills and keeping an accurate record of your expenditures. Use of credit cards ceases to be a blessing, however, when you are unable to pay your bills in full and must pay interest of at least 18 percent. Another potential liability of plastic credit is the possible temptation to buy things you would not purchase otherwise.

To keep a good credit rating, you will need to maintain active credit accounts and keep them current—never becoming delinquent with a payment. By paying bills promptly, you will be able to obtain a major loan at a reasonable interest rate when you need it.

Planning Insurance Coverage

You and your bride should make decisions about insuring your life, her life, your automobile, home, and other property. You may need to expand existing coverage or change the beneficiary on policies you now hold.

There are companies specializing in each of the above areas and others offer "total" coverage. There are salesmen who represent only one firm and agents who represent several companies. Those representing several firms claim the advantage of ability to write your insurance with the company they feel is best able to meet your needs. We suggest that you get proposals from two or three companies before you and your partner make a final decision. Be sure to investigate insurance and savings programs where you work.

Making a Will

Although it may seem that your assets are few, it's a good practice to see a lawyer about a will for you and your wife. It's smart estate planning to draw up a will now and then have it updated as your assets and circumstances change.

Monthly Household Budget

Income
    Gross Monthly Pay (combined) _____
    Federal Taxes Withheld _____
    Other Taxes Withheld _____
    Other Withholding _____
    Total Withholding _____
    Take Home Income _____

Emergency Fund
    Balance for Living Expenses
    and Savings Account _____

Living Expenses
    Rent or Mortgage _____
    Utilities _____
    Other Taxes (property, etc.) _____
    Food and Household Needs _____
    Insurance (Life, Health, Auto) _____
    Automobile Payment _____
    Automobile Expenses _____
    Clothing _____
    Medical-Dental Expense _____
    Contributions _____
    Entertainment-Recreation _____
    Christmas Gifts, etc. _____
    Personal Allowances _____
    Total Living Expenses _____
Savings Account _____

Timetable for the Groom

While the groom traditionally has fewer wedding responsibilities than the bride, your involvement is most vital. The timetable below spans six months but may be accomplished in less time in smaller communities. Couples living near large cities may need from eight months to a year to plan. Adapt the checklist to fit your needs. Remember, however, that the faster things are done, the less pressure you will be put under.

Six Months Before

- _____ Order bride's engagement ring and wedding band
- _____ Settle on type of wedding, including time and place, with your fiancée
- _____ Start preparing your guest list
- _____ Arrange to visit minister or other officiant
- _____ Discuss financing of wedding with fiancée, all parents
- _____ Think about who you'd like as groomsmen
- _____ Discuss honeymoon plans with bride-to-be and begin making reservations
- _____ Check on passports, visas and inoculations if traveling abroad

Three Months Before

- _____ Discuss all wedding preparations with fiancée
- _____ Complete the guest list; give to fiancée
- _____ Confirm participation of best man and ushers
- _____ Order your wedding attire and advise groomsmen in ordering theirs
- _____ Get honeymoon plans in order
- _____ Assist parents in arranging rehearsal dinner
- _____ Arrange lodging for relatives and groomsmen from out of town

One Month Before

- _____ Pick up bride's wedding ring; check engraving
- _____ Decide on bride's bouquet and going-away corsage; check with fiancée on mothers' corsages and boutonnieres for men
- _____ Check on lodging for out-of-town attendants
- _____ Select gifts for your bride, attendants

_____ Make sure necessary legal and medical documents are in order
_____ Make certain groomsmen have ordered their clothing
_____ Look over personal wardrobe; discard worn out clothing

Two Weeks Before

_____ Make a date with fiancée to get license
_____ Assist parents in completing preparations for rehearsal dinner
_____ Check on arrangements for the bachelor party
_____ Arrange with best man for transportation from reception to airport (or other departure point)
_____ Double check on honeymoon reservations

One Week Before

_____ Arrange to present gifts to best man and ushers at bachelor party or rehearsal dinner
_____ Remind groomsmen of wedding rehearsal
_____ Arrange for any special seating at the ceremony
_____ Double check on plans for bachelor party and rehearsal dinner
_____ Put clergyman's fee in envelope; deliver envelope and marriage license to best man
_____ Finish packing for the honeymoon
_____ Be sure your car is in good condition for travel
_____ Check on auto or trip insurance as needed

On Your Wedding Day

_____ Check with best man early (possibly for breakfast) or meet groomsmen for brunch if time permits; make certain everything is in readiness
_____ Call your bride-to-be and reassure her
_____ Deliver bride's wedding band to best man
_____ Arrive at church with best man a full hour before ceremony if fully dressed; give yourself an hour and a half if you are dressing at the church

Quick Reference Index

Accommodations for guests, 38, 68
Aisle carpet, 25, 54
Album, photo, 49
Altar procedures, 58
Announcement of engagement,
  by bride's parents, 4
  through newspapers, 31
Attendance, estimating, 27
Attendants, 23-26
  bridal, 10-11, 23
  contacting, 24
  gifts for, 44
  groom's, 23-26
  honor, 23-24
Automobile, going-away, 25

Bachelor dinner, party, 37-38
  alternatives to, 38, 68
  planning for, 37-38
Benediction, choral, 20
Best man
  duties of, 24-25, 54, 56, 57, 59-60
  father as, 14, 23
  selection of, 23
Bills, paying the, 66-70
  in advance, 38-48
  promptly, 66
Bouquets, wedding, *see also* Flowers
  attendants', 40
  bride's, 40-41
Boutonnieres, 41
Bridal consultant, 34
Bridal service, 42
Bride
  attendants and the, 14, 26
  flowers and the, 40
  "giving away" of, 58
  groom's support of, 12, 56
  luncheon for, 15, 37
  musicians and, 19
  planning with groom, 8-12
  and preserving memories, 47
  and wedding gown, 9
Bride's home, 43
Bridesmaids, 14, 26
  dresses for, 14
Brother,
  bride's, 11
  groom's, 15
Budget,
  groom's wedding, 69-70
  household, 74

Cake, wedding, 59
Candles
  lighting of, 25
  unity, 17, 18
Caterer
  church hostess as, 68
  negotiating with, 52
  for rehearsal dinner, 52
Ceremony, wedding
  altar procedures, 58
  civil, 17
  composing vows, 11, 18
  conference with minister and, 11, 17
  double-ring, 11
  processional, 19
  recessional, 20
  rehearsal of, 11, 54
  selection of, 17
  single-ring, 11
Checking account, 73
Checklist, groom's, 75-76
Church building, 10
Church hostess, 52
Civil ceremony, 17
Clergyman, *see* Minister, Officiant
Clippings, newspaper, 31
Clothes, wedding,
  bride's, 8, 9
  bridesmaids, 14, 44
  business suit, 9, 34
  coordinating, 9, 15
  fathers', 36
  formal, 34
  groom's 9, 34-36
  informal, 9
  local custom and, 34
  men's, 8, 9, 34-36
  minister's, 36
  mothers', 15
  protecting, 36
  ushers', 35
  very formal, 9, 35
credit, controling, 73
cues, wedding, 54, 55, *see also*
  Rehearsal, wedding

Date of wedding, 9
Daytime wedding, 9, 35
Dinner,
  bachelor, 37-38
  rehearsal, 51-53
Doctor's certificate, 21
Dress, wedding, 9, *see also*
  Clothes, wedding.

Dresses,
  bridesmaids', 14, 44
  mothers', 15
  street-length, 9
Director, wedding, 54
Dressing at home, 76
Dressing at wedding site, 76

Emergency fund, 72, 74
Engagement, announcement of
  by bride's parents, 4
  at engagement party, 4
  in newspapers, 4
  telling bride's parents, 3-4
  telling groom's parents, 4
Engagement ring
  for bride, 4-6
  for groom, 7
  purchasing, 4-6
Entertaining, 37-39
  bride, 4
  bride and groom, 4
  bride's parents, 4
  groomsmen, 37-38
  out-of-town guests, 38
Enjoying the wedding, 56
Episcopal wedding service, 18
Estimating attendance, 27
Evening wedding, 9
Expenses, *see also* Paying the bills.
  wedding, 11, 66-67
  attendants', 12, 67
  bride and family, 11, 66-67
  budgeting for, 69-70
  cutting, 67-69
  groom and family, 11, 67
  sharing, 11, 14

Family
  bride's, 11, 27, 60, 65
  groom's, 13-16, 27
Father
  of the bride, 36, 58
  of the groom, 14, 36
Fathers' dress, 36
Fee, minister's, 57, 76
Fiancee, planning with, 3, 8-11
Financing the, *see also* Expenses,
  wedding,
  wedding, 11-12, 66-70
Financial planning, 7, 72-74
Florist, selecting a, 40
Flowers,
  bouquets, 40-41
  boutonnieres, 41
  corsages for mothers, 41
  ordering, 41
  for reception, 40
  for rehearsal dinner, 53
  throwing bouquet, 59
  for wedding ceremony, 40
Foreign travel, 22, 62
Formality, relative, 9
Formal wear, men's 9, 34-35
Formal wedding, 8-9

Garden wedding, 10
Garter, bride's, 59
Get-together
  for out-of-town guests, 38
  for parents of bride and groom, 4
Gifts
  acknowledgement of, 43
  arrival of, 43
  for attendants, 44
  displaying, 43
  duplicate, 71
  exchanging, 71
  from groom's friends, 43
  for the home, 42
  labeling of, 43
  photographs as, 49
  recording of, 43
  thank-you-notes for, 43
Gift registry, 42
Gift table, 43
"Giving away" of bride, 58
Gown, wedding, 9
Grandparents, 15
Groom
  and arranging honeymoon, 61-65
  and family obligations, 13-16
  and financial planning, 7, 11, 72-73
  and planning with family, 13-16
  and planning with fiancée, 8-12
  and purchasing rings, 4-6
  and preserving memories, 47-50
  and selecting gifts, 43-44
  and selecting groomsmen, 23-24
  and saving money, 67-69
  and selecting flowers, 41-42
  and wardrobe planning, 45-46
  and wedding clothing, 34-35
  and wedding timetable, 75
Guest list,
  compiling, 27-28
  reducing, 28
Guests, wedding
  accommodations for, 38-68
  entertaining out-of-town, 37, 38

and the reception, 58-59
response to invitations, 52
seating at ceremony, 25

Head usher, 27
Home,
  bride's, 43
  groom's, 15, 16
Home wedding, 10
Honeymoon, 61-65
  avoiding exhausting, 61
  best man and, 25, 59, 61, 64
  in Caribbean, 62
  deferring the, 64
  in Europe, 62
  photographing the, 64-65
  in Poconos, 62-63
  purpose of, 61
  in recreational vehicle, 64
  saving money and, 63-64, 69
  in state parks, 63
  in South Carolina, 63-64
  tipping and, 64
  travel agent and, 63
  in vacation cottage, 64
  weekend, 64
Honor attendants, 24
Host, wedding, 8
Hotels, motels, 38

Informal wedding, 9
Invitations, wedding, 28-30
  addressing, 28
  compiling guest list for, 27-28
  mailing of, 28
  pictorial, 30
  printing of, 28
  selection of, 28
  titles and, 28
  wording of, 28-30
Insurance, 7, 74

Jeweler, 5-7
J M Productions, Inc., 18

Knight, George W., 18

Legal requirements, 21-22
License, marriage, 21-22
Lodging for out-of-town guests, 38-39
Luggage
  Packing, 46, 57
  Selecting, 46

Maid of honor, 23
Managing money, 72-73
Marriage commitment, 3, 12, 56
Matron of honor, 23
Memory box, bride's, 31
Men's formal wear, see clothing,
  wedding,
Menu, rehearsal dinner, 52
Minister, 10, 11, 17, 18, 58, see also
  Pastor, Officiant
  fee for, 57
  clothing for, 36
  conference with, 11, 17
Mother,
  of the bride, 15, 58
  of the groom, 14, 15
Music, 18-20, 53
  anthems, 19
  choral, 20
  classical, 19
  contemporary, 19, 53
  instrumental, 19
  popular, 19, 53
  planning for, 18-19
  processional, 19-20
  at Protestant weddings, 19
  recessional, 20
  at rehearsal dinner, 53
  traditional, 19
  vocal, 20
Musicians, 18-20, 53
  choir director, 19
  organist, 19
  pianist, 19
  soloist, 20

Newspaper announcements, 4, 31-33
  of the engagement, 4, 31-32
  of the wedding, 32-33

Officiant, wedding, 10-11, 17-18, 58,
  see also Minister, Pastor
Organist, 19
Outdoor wedding, 10
Out-of-town groom, 39, 53
Out-of-town guests, 38

Paying the bills, 66-70, see also
  Expenses, wedding
Parents
  bride's, 3, 4
  engagement and, 4
  expenses and, 11, 14, 66-67
  groom's, 4, 13-16
  informing of engagement, 3-4

Parties,
   for bride, 15
   for groom, 43
   for groomsmen, 15, 37, 38, 39, 57
Pastor, *see also* Minister.
   bride's, 10
   groom's, 10
Photographer, 47-49
   negotiating with, 48
   paying, 48
   selecting a, 48
Photographs
   bridal portrait, 48
   candid, 49
   formal, 48, 49
   gifts of, 49
   for newspapers, 48
Pictures, *see* Photographs.
Place of Wedding, 10
Processional, 19-20, 58
Program, printed wedding, 49-50
Protestant wedding, 18, 19
Public address system, 18
Publicity, wedding, *see* Newspaper announcements.

Receiving line,
   formal, 58, 59
   informal, 58
Reception, 51, 58-59
   garden, 10
   home, 10
   location of, 10
   receiving line, 59
   stand-up, 59
   throwing bouquet and garter at, 59
   toasts at, 59
Recessional, 20, 25, 58
Recording the ceremony, 49
Reducing guest list, 28
Rehearsal dinner, 51-53
   caterer for, 52
   guests for, 51
   host of, 38, 51
   location of, 52
   music for, 53
   program for, 52-53
   seating for, 53
Rehearsal, wedding, 54-55
   absence from, 54
   bride and, 54-55
   bride's mother and, 54
   confusion and, 55
   direction of, 54
   entrance cues, 54, 55
   exit cues, 54, 55
   groom and, 54
   groom's parents and, 55

   purpose of, 54
   time of, 54
Rental, formal clothes, 35
Response to invitation, 52
Rice, throwing, 59
Rings, engagement
   for bride, 4-6
   for groom, 7
Rings, wedding
   for bride, 5-6
   for groom, 5, 6-7

Saving money, 67-69
   on bachelor dinner, 38, 68
   on engagement ring, 6, 68
   on gifts, 69
   on honeymoon, 62, 63-64, 69
   on lodging, 15, 68
   on luggage, 46
   on musicians, 19
   on rehearsal dinner, 52, 68
   on wedding clothes, 68
Saying Goodbye
   to groomsmen, 59
   to parents, 59
Seating arrangements
   for mothers, 25, 58
   at reception, 24, 26
   at rehearsal dinner, 53
   for wedding guests, 25
Shoes, wedding
   protecting, 36
   selection of, 34, 35
Showers
   for bride, 15
   for groom, 37
Sister
   of the bride, 24
   of the groom, 15
Size of wedding, 8, 10, 27, 67
Sponsor of wedding, 29
Stand-in bride at rehearsal, 54-55
Symbolism, wedding, 17

Telegram to bride's parents, 60
Telephoning
   bride on wedding day, 56
   bride's parents, 4, 65
   groom's parents, 13, 65
Thank-you notes, 43
Throwing bridal bouquet, 59
Time of wedding, 8, 9
   afternoon, 8, 34, 35
   evening, 8, 9, 35
Timetable, groom's, 75-76
Titles, 28
Toasts, 24, 26

   at rehearsal dinner, 52
   at wedding reception, 59
Traditions, wedding, 17
Transportation, 12, 66
   to ceremony, 12, 67
   on honeymoon, 25, 59, 69
Traveling by air, 61

Unity candle, 17-18
Undergarments, groom's, 46
Ushers, 23-26
   clothes for, 34, 35
   duties of, 25-26
   gifts for, 44
   head of, 25
   selection of 23-24
Utilities, 7, 71

Vacation, groom's 12
Videotaping the wedding, 50
Vows, 17, 18, 58
   composing, 11, 18
   memorizing, 11, 18

Walking Horse Hotel, 39
Wardrobe, groom's, 45-46
   Choosing luggage, 46
   Discarding worn clothes, 45
   packing for honeymoon, 45-46
   selection and planning, 45-46
Wedding
   civil, 17
   evening, 9
   formal, 9
   home, 10
   informal, 8, 9
   location of, 10
   out-of-town, 38, 39, 66
   very formal, 9
Wedding day, 56-60
   breakfast with best man on, 56
   brunch for groomsmen on, 57
   enjoying the 56-60
   good night's sleep and, 56
Wedding day checklist, 76
"White tie," 9
Will, making a, 74

Notes

See page 11
page 24 Best man duties

Notes

Notes

Notes

Notes

Notes

Notes